Praise for *Paychecks for Life*

For 30 years, Charlie Epstein has been one of the most respected and innovative thinkers in the retirement industry. In *Paychecks for Life*, he attacks the problem of lifetime income with the creative mindset that is his hallmark.

Mike Alfred
CEO, Brightscope

Paychecks for Life is the best financial planning guide I've ever seen in my years as a pension consultant and financial planner. Without backing away from the real complexities of the financial world, Charlie provides a fun and easy-to-understand blueprint for success. This book should be required reading in every high school in America.

Pete Swisher, CFP®, CPC
Author of *401(k) Fiduciary Governance: An Advisor's Guide*

Charlie is one of the brightest and most creative people in this business. *Paychecks for Life* contains valuable ideas that will help anyone on his or her journey to a successful "desirement."

Ted Benna,
"The Father of the 401(k)"
CEO, Malvern Benefits Corp.
Author of *401(k) for Dummies*

Once upon a time, our parents were promised a "paycheck for life" in return for giving their working years to one company. Those days are gone. Charlie Epstein revives the hope of a paycheck for life for every American worker with his practical, street-smart guidance based on real-life experiences. If his nine principles for retirement saving were taught in our schools, they'd jumpstart our society's financial literacy.

John Scott
The401kExpert.com

Charlie Epstein has a simple idea: Make sure everyone in America is absolutely clear on how to get a paycheck for the rest of their lives. He knows exactly how a person can achieve this security, no matter what happens in the world or in the markets. America will be a much more confident and prosperous country if 100 million people read this book and put the Paychecks for Life strategy into practice.

Dan Sullivan
Founder, Strategic Coach®

i

Paychecks for Life takes the advisor jargon out of retirement planning. A great resource for people who want to retire successfully but get lost in the language of financial planning.

Edward Dressel
President, Trust Builders, Inc.

Planning for retirement can be a daunting process. In *Paychecks for Life*, Charlie Epstein has cracked the code and developed a simple yet effective approach that every American worker can use. Follow his nine principles and you'll achieve a successful retirement savings process that will serve you for a lifetime.

Donald B. Trone
Chief Ethos Officer, 3ethos

Paychecks for Life is classic Charlie Epstein: A delightful blend of real-life examples and insightful humor.

Craig L. Israelsen, Ph.D.
Author of *7Twelve: A Diversified Investment Portfolio with a Plan*

In *Paychecks for Life*, Charlie Epstein shares valuable ideas that can help turn your dreams into reality. He cuts through the fog so you can enjoy your ride to retirement savings with confidence. A tool worth referring to again and again.

Gerald J. Wernette, CPA, CEBS, AIFA
Principal/Director, Rehmann Retirement Builders
Rehmann Financial

For better or worse, America has shifted primary responsibility for ensuring adequate retirement income to the individual worker. As a result, there's an urgent need for investment education—and *Paychecks for Life* answers the call. Translating technical knowledge into terms that anyone can understand, the book succinctly explains everything from automating your 401k to the intricacies of plan fees and expenses. Truly a welcome addition to the literature on 401(k)s.

Marcia S. Wagner, Esq.
Managing Director, The Wagner Law Group

I've read dozens of books on financial and retirement planning. While most other books provide good technical knowledge, *Paychecks for Life* is the first book I've encountered that provides a clear, concise and systematic approach to reaching a successful retirement. Charlie Epstein does a wonderful job of making retirement planning less daunting.

Jud Doherty, CFA
President, Stadion Money Management

Retirement calculations and actuarial concepts can be very complex and beyond the ability of many non-financial individuals to grasp. *Paychecks for Life* makes retirement saving simple to understand and provides a clear roadmap that can be followed to successful completion. If everyone in America followed these steps, the country would be in much better financial shape.

Gregory W. Kasten, MD, MBA, CFP®, CPC, AIFA®
CEO, Unified Trust Company

Paychecks for Life should be required reading for every American worker. Charlie Epstein takes complicated investment and savings concepts and breaks them down into nine easy-to-understand principles. The book is not only entertaining but full of strategies that anyone can implement immediately to improve their financial future.

Dan Kravitz
President, Kravitz Inc.

Finally, a book that spells out in plain English how to save for retirement (or should I say "desirement"). Charlie Epstein nails it by sharing actionable, realistic steps that anyone can use to achieve a dignified exit from the rat race. I can't wait to share *Paychecks for Life* with my family, friends and clients.

James F. Sampson, AIF®
Managing Principal, Cornerstone Retirement Advisors, LLC

Paychecks for Life

HOW TO TURN YOUR 401(K) INTO A PAYCHECK MANUFACTURING COMPANY

Charles D. Epstein

THE 401K COACH®

401k Coach LLC
Holyoke, MA

Paychecks for Life Disclaimer

This book is designed to provide accurate and authoritative information on the subject of personal finances. While all of the stories and anecdotes described in the book are based on true experiences, most of the names are pseudonyms, and some situations have been changed slightly for educational purposes and to protect privacy. This book is sold with the understanding that the Author is not engaged in rendering legal, accounting, or other professional services by publishing this book. As each individual situation is unique, questions relevent to personal finances and specific to the individual should be addressed directly with an appropriate professional to ensure that the situation has been evaluated carefully and appropriately. The Author specifically disclaims any liability, loss or risk which is incurred as a consequence, whether direct or indirect, of the use and application of any of the contents of this work.

ISBN 978-0-9836246-3-9 (hardcover)
ISBN 978-0-9836246-4-6 (softcover)

Publisher's Cataloging-in-Publication data

Epstein, Charles D.
    Paychecks for life : how to turn your 401k into a paycheck manufacturing company / Charles D. Epstein.
    p. cm.
    Includes bibliographical references and index.
    ISBN 978-0-9836246-3-9 (Hardcover)
    ISBN 978-0-9836246-4-6 (pbk.)
    ISBN 978-0-9836246-5-3 (ebook)
1. 401(k) plans. 2. Retirement income—Planning. 3. Retirement—Planning. 4. Financial planning. 5. Finance, Personal. 6. Portfolio management —United States. I. Title.

HD7105.4.E67 2011
332.024/01—dc22   2011930141

First Edition

Copies of this book may be purchased for educational, business or promotional use. For information, please call (877) 932-6236 or send email to info@the401kcoach.com.

401K Coach LLC
330 Whitney Ave, Suite 610
Holyoke, MA 01040

Printed in the U.S.A.

This book is dedicated to America's 401(k) participants
and the belief that paychecks for life are within your reach.

Table of Contents

Acknowledgements

This book represents the culmination of a lifetime of learning and in-the-trenches exploration of many financial ideas and concepts throughout my thirty-one-year professional career as a financial service advisor and The 401k Coach. The result is a synthesis of the best of these ideas and concepts into the "Paychecks for Life system": nine core principles for building a Paycheck Manufacturing Company out of your employer's 401(k) plan.

For my lifetime of learning, I owe deep thanks to many individuals who influenced my thinking and success. First, to all my teachers and professors, especially those great ones: Mrs. Schechter, my fourth-grade teacher, who sparked my interest in numbers and encouraged me to think for myself; Mr. Gatchel, who in tenth-grade geometry demonstrated, every day, that learning could be fun and entertaining; Hugh Pinchin, my Colgate economics professor and honors advisor, who turned me on to the power of the multiplier effect, the eighth wonder of the world; and finally Mary Doyle, my first-year Meisner acting teacher who taught me that less is more.

To my business mentors: Hillard Aronson, who was there from the beginning, prodding me to success and teaching me that "no never means never, it just means not now"; Werner Erhard, who gave me the experience of transformation; and Dan Sullivan, The Strategic Coach, who is the best coach an entrepreneur could ask for: thanks for the courage you have demonstrated all these years to follow your inner voice and wisdom when I'm sure many doubts existed. You have inspired my success and created a great laboratory to test out my instincts and bring The 401k Coach and *Paychecks for Life* to life! And to Ted Benna, who started it all—thanks for the spark.

To the team of dedicated individuals at Epstein Financial Services and The 401k Coach, Lynne Peluso, Lisa Thompson, Sue Bader, Marie Forest, Amanda Walker, Betty Jean Bouffard, Sheldon Snodgrass, Danielle Hall, Leo Polverini, Peter Riggins and Barbara Lewis: thank you all for your continued belief in our work and my vision. Whatever success I have is a direct reflection of your efforts. Special thanks to Jeff McEwen, founding partner of The 401k Coach, who was there in the beginning, over tuna fish sandwiches at Romito's, and to Hillary Durcharme ("The

Dog"), our first employee who single-handedly made every workshop possible in those early years. Also, to Pete Novak, a friend for life and supporter of my business, thanks for watching my back. Everyone should be blessed with you as their General Agent.

I'm grateful to the hundreds of personal clients who have entrusted me and my team at Epstein Financial Services with their financial futures and have benefited from our collective financial wisdom.

As The 401k Coach, I have been privileged to have benefited from interacting with and learning from the thousands of financial advisors across the country who have participated in our coaching programs. To all, a heartfelt thanks for allowing me to share and test my ideas with you. Your feedback and continued confidence in our work is greatly appreciated.

There have been many financial institutions, executives, and internal and external wholesalers who have risked sponsoring our 401k Coach programs over the past nine years. Without your support, I wouldn't have had the luxury of testing these ideas in the trenches with advisors across the country.

To Gary Kleinschmitt of Legg Mason, The 401k Coach's first advocate, you were there when it was just an idea. Your support paved the way for the Coach to launch and gain traction. I am forever indebted to your ongoing support. To Jeff Atwell, Kelly Elder, and Rick Klunk, who put us on the road and on the map in Texas, thanks for taking a chance with me.

To all those financial organizations who have sponsored The 401k Coach—Michael Butler of Nationwide; Rick Mason, Lou Bachetti, and Bill Elmsley of ING; Shefali Desai and Hugh O'Toole of Mass Mutual; Paul Swanson, Peter Simms, and Mike Conte of Lincoln; and Ryan Bauer, Chuck Lombardo, and Mike Ziccardi of Mutual Omaha. A man could ask for no better partners in the quest to create paychecks for life for every 401(k) participant.

To all the mutual fund companies who have sponsored The 401k Coach Program, I am forever grateful. Special thanks to Jamie Fox at Delaware for your continued advocacy and Matt Schoneman at TRA for your belief in the value of our program for your customers.

To the team at HighSpot, thanks for keeping me pointed in the right direction.

To the Epsteins—my grandfather Max, the accountant, and my dad, Bob, the executive—both of you were entrepreneurs in your day and knew the risk and thrill of building businesses. Thanks for instilling in me that same passion, drive, and work ethic. To the Burtaines—Henry, my grandfather, the artist and musician, and Peggy, my mother, the opera singer and pianist—you gave me the spirit and zeal to find my voice and the desire to entertain everyone. To my children, Hannah and Noah, you inspire me every day. Even when I'm on the road, I'm thinking of you and am there for you. And lastly, to my loving wife, Lorie: thank you for hitting me with your car that fateful day and waking me up! You are forever my spirit; there's no one else. I love you.

Introduction

Good Morning America!
Your Paychecks Have Stopped

Despite the early mornings, long hours, short lunches, co-worker conflicts, customer complaints, rush-hour traffic jams, and pointless meetings with people who have been promoted past their competency, you continue to battle with that dreaded thing called work for one reason only: a paycheck.

It's a lot to endure for so little in return. To make things worse, the government helps itself to a generous share—perhaps 28% or more—of your hard-earned dollars, making you wonder if it's even worth the trouble. Yet you continue to work for that paycheck. It's essential for survival.

If the everyday routine seems unsettling, let's look at the alternative. Imagine for a moment that your paychecks stop—not just for a week or a month, but forever. What would you do? How would you survive?

Perhaps you're thinking it's not going to happen. Perhaps you're thinking it's best not to think about it.

Well, you should, because you'll retire one day, and when that day comes, no matter how far away it may be, the paychecks will stop. It's not a matter of *if*, it's a matter of *when*.

The Paychecks for Life Inverted Pyramid

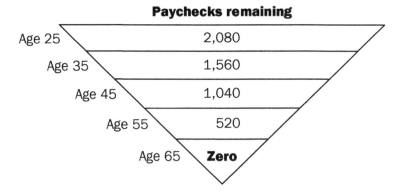

Paychecks remaining

Age 25	2,080
Age 35	1,560
Age 45	1,040
Age 55	520
Age 65	**Zero**

Consider the "Paychecks for Life Inverted Pyramid" above. At age twenty-five, assuming you're paid every week for fifty-two weeks, you'll have 2,080 (52 weeks × 40 years) paychecks remaining until age sixty-five. At age thirty-five, you'll have 1,560 (52 weeks × 30 years) paychecks remaining. And so on until age sixty-five, when you'll have *zero* paychecks left. What will happen when that day comes?

You don't think your boss is going to reward you with a lifetime of checks for all your hard work, do you? Of course not. After all, his retirement package is *you*. He's the entrepreneur. He's the one who's been taking risks with his money every day. He's the one who's been using your labor to build a business he can sell one day and then sail off into the sunset to enjoy *his* retirement. He's the one gladly paying you a steady paycheck now in exchange for not having to worry about receiving one in the future. You, as an employee, don't have the same luxury. You, as an employee, will have to plan how to survive without that monthly check. Consider the chilling fact that you may live almost as long without a paycheck as with one. According to the 2010 Social

Security Administration Period Life Tables, in the last sixty years, mean life expectancy has risen by ten years, from sixty-eight years in 1950 to seventy-eight years in 2010. And if you make it to age sixty-five, your life expectancy is extended to eighty-three if you're a man and eighty-five if you're a women.

Consider the chilling fact that you may live almost as long without a paycheck as with one.

The question you need to answer today is: Will I have the resources to support my current lifestyle once the paychecks stop? "Ah! But!" I hear you saying. "There's Social Security. The government will take care of me."

Don't count on it.

The Social Security Administration (SSA) is expected to be nearly bankrupt by 2037. According to a 2010 report from the SSA, it will begin paying more in benefits than it collects in revenue by 2015, and will need to begin tapping its trust funds to support monthly payments. Unless there's some major intervention, the trust funds will be depleted by 2037 and the SSA will be able to pay only 76% of promised benefits.

At best, Social Security was designed only to supplement other sources of income. President Franklin D. Roosevelt signed the original law in 1935 as part of his New Deal (the name he gave to a complex number of packages designed to give relief, institute reform, and aid recovery during the Great Depression) to combat unemployment and poverty and reduce the burden on workers not eligible for retirement packages. In fact, the formal acronym for Social Security is OASDI, which stands for Old Age, Survivors, and Disability Insurance. It's an entitlement program, a right granted through law. It's not a welfare program.

Even if you're lucky enough to receive a Social Security check upon retirement, you'll be on the endangered species list. The money you receive will barely cover the cost of basic essentials. That's the supply side of the story. There's a demand side as well. Your monthly monetary requirements often increase when you retire because you have more time for vacations, cruises, golf, tennis, dinners, movies, and, of course, mandatory visits to see the grandchildren. Every day could be a weekend, with higher demands for money.

So what are you going to do? Well, you have two choices. You can retire and do nothing all day, or you can retire and do all the things you really want to do. The things you've worked so hard for. The things you've always dreamed about. For that, you'll need additional money. But where will you get it? You can't continue to work forever. And you can't build a business you can sell someday—or can you?

What if I told you that you can build a business that will give you a steady stream of secure monthly paychecks? That while your boss may not directly pay for your retirement, his or her company's 401(k) plan can, if you let it?

I know what you're thinking: "My 401(k), Charlie? You mean the one I have at work? That thing? What's all the fuss about? For years I put money in my 401(k) plan, but in 2008 it was reduced to a 201(k)."

Yes, that 401(k). If you lend me the time it will take to read this book, I promise I'll give you the financial clarity, confidence, and capabilities you need to turn that ol 401(k) plan of yours into a Paycheck Manufacturing Company. You can use this system right now to set yourself back on the path to financial independence and reduced financial anxiety.

My name is Charles Epstein, and I'm going to show you how. Over the past thirty-one years as a financial advisor and as The 401k Coach to thousands of financial professionals across the country, I've discovered nine powerful financial principles that everyone can use to create a steady stream of secure monthly retirement income—paychecks for life. While your boss may not directly pay for your retirement, his or her company's 401(k) plan gives you a method to take care of it yourself.

The process is easy. I teach it to clients every day, and I'll teach it to you over the course of this book.

Your Annual Eviction Notices

Annual Eviction Notice #1: Social Security

"You have hereby been served notice of eviction." Yes, you! Unlike most evictions, though, this one is not readily apparent to you or your neighbors. The sheriff didn't leave an ominous notice at the door. Your furniture and personal belongings are not at the curb. The lights are still on, the cable television is working, and your cat isn't clinging to the drapes from all the commotion. And, unlike normal eviction notices, you're not being evicted for failure to pay. You're being evicted because of the government's failure to pay.

That's right. The government serves you with an annual notice saying that it will no longer be able to make the Social Security payments it has promised to you. In addition, you're getting kicked out of the system. Yes, I know, you were required to pay into the system—a lot—and in return you were guaranteed full benefits at retirement. Now those payments are in jeopardy of being drastically reduced.

Where is this eviction notice displayed? Believe it or not, it's right there on your Social Security statement. Naturally, when you receive the statement, you're so anxious to see the surprise dollars inside that there's no time to read the small print. Instead, you jump directly to page two and check your estimated benefits at ages sixty-two, sixty-seven, and seventy. Upon seeing some respectable dollar figures, you breathe a big sigh of relief and pitch the statement into your files. It appears to be money in the bank, and that's all you need to know.

But if you look closely at the first page, you'll see the following notice:

> *Social Security is a compact between generations. Since 1935, America has kept the promise of security for its workers and their families. Now, however, the Social Security system is facing serious financial problems, and action is needed soon to make sure the system will be sound when today's younger workers are ready for retirement. In 2015, we will begin paying more in benefits than we collect in taxes. Without changes, by 2037 the Social Security Trust Fund will be able to pay only about 76 cents for each dollar of scheduled benefits. We need to resolve these issues soon to make sure Social Security continues to provide a foundation of protection for future generations.*

You didn't do anything wrong, but you shouldn't expect full benefits. If your retirement is a long way away, it's probably safe to say you shouldn't expect any benefits at all. You still have to pay into the system as if you're going to receive full benefits, but the government has put you on notice that you're on your own to make up for any shortfalls.

Check Your Earnings Record

I'd like to point out another important section on your earnings statement. On page three, the SSA states that you, your employer, and the SSA share responsibility for the accuracy of your earnings record. If you're now expected to receive only 76% of your benefits from Social Security, make sure the benefits you're eligible for are the highest they can be.

According to the SSA, it's the highest 35 years of earnings and your last three years, not the taxes you paid, that determine your social security benefits. If the records incorrectly show lower earnings than you actually had, your payments may be reduced. So while you're reading the eviction notice on your next Social Security statement, also be sure to take a peek at your reported earnings statement on page three. Make sure it is accurate by comparing the government's numbers with your actual earnings. If you spot any errors, contact your local SSA office to have them corrected.

Annual Eviction Notice #2: Pension Plans

"You have hereby been served notice of eviction."

What?! Again? Now what?

Social Security is not the only plan serving eviction notices. Pension plans, which are a type of corporate retirement plan, are busy leaving eviction notices with unsuspecting employees. In 2007, of all the Fortune 500 pension plans that existed in 1996, 25% had been terminated, closed or frozen. Between 1996 and 2007, Fortune 500 plans were closed or frozen at the average rate of 3% per year. In 2006, Verizon and IBM shocked the corporate world by freezing their pension plans (managers only, in the case of Verizon), which created a standard that others soon followed. That same year, 8.2% of pension funds were either closed or frozen, creating the largest percentage drop since 1996. In 2008, Hewitt Consulting (now Aon Hewitt) reported that if the average decline that had occurred since 2002 continued (something the company considers unlikely), there will be no more open-plan pension funds in the Fortune 500 by 2019. Most employees who have pension plans will accrue no more benefits while future employees will receive none.

Social Security and pension plans are nothing but promises that can obviously be broken. No matter how long you've been paying into Social Security or employed at your job, your benefits are not as secure as they appear. They're essentially pledges that if everything goes well for the next twenty or thirty years, *then* you'll receive the promised benefits. That's a long time, especially with all the financial instability in the world right now. It's not a wise choice to bank on Social Security or pension plans to support you after you stop working.

The good news about your 401(k) plan is that you always know where you stand. It's your money, in your account, managed for your benefit. My friends, you need to start maximizing this program by making contributions and begin building a business that can generate paychecks for life.

Linda and Jerry Stevens

The Millionaires Next Door

Back in 1988, when Linda and Jerry first entered my office, it seemed the world's economy was ready to collapse as the credit crisis worsened and the world's governments scrambled to find a way to avert the greatest economic crisis since the Great Depression. The U.S. economy was teetering on the brink of calamity. Black Monday had struck in October 1987, and now the U.S. banking system was in danger of collapsing. It certainly didn't seem like the right time to begin investing.

Back then, Jerry was a forty-year-old manufacturing representative making $40,000 per year; Linda was thirty-five years old and earning $30,000 per year as an office administrator. They had two children: Jacqueline, age twelve, and Randy, ten.

When we met to review their progress in December 2008—twenty years later—similar economic news was circulating. Across the United States, banks and major Wall Street firms were closing their doors as the world faced a global credit crisis and U.S. stock markets were plummeting, losing 43% of their value in six months. It was financial déjà vu. But in contrast to the daily news reports that the sky was falling and that millions of Americans were watching their retirement savings go down the drain, Jerry and Linda sat calmly in my office, smiling warmly as we reminisced about our twenty-year journey together.

"I'll never forget the first time we met," laughed Jerry, looking at Linda and then at me. "I thought you were a lunatic! You were sitting there talking about paychecks for life and our desirement years, and I was looking over at Linda thinking, 'What kind of crazy salesman has she dragged me off to listen to this time?'"

"Yes, that's me," chuckled Linda, "always dragging Jerry off to crazies.

"But seriously," she continued, "I had been to several meetings about our 401(k) plan since I started working as an office manager at my company in 1982. I had never contributed to the plan, for two main reasons. First, every time I went to one of the 401(k) meetings, I couldn't understand a single thing the financial person was saying. It was all gobbledygook to me. I'd walk out of there more confused than when I'd walked in. And second..."

Before Linda could finish, Jerry jumped in: "Second, I was adamantly against the 401(k) plan."

"Oh yes, I remember how adamant you were when we first met," I lamented. "Boy, do I remember."

"Yeah, we had some wonderful debates that first year we started working with you," Jerry smiled, remembering.

"Wonderful for you," I corrected. "Heated for me."

"You got us thinking about our financial future," Linda continued, "what we were doing, and, more importantly, what we *weren't* doing. You made us stretch our imaginations and picture a 'bigger financial future' for ourselves; you made us think about our dreams, our aspirations, and what we really want to do after we stop working in our chosen professions and start living our desirement years. After you calculated what those dreams would cost, we created a desirement mortgage for ourselves and turned our companies' 401(k) plans into our very own Paycheck Manufacturing Companies. I became a born-again 401(k) participant," she finished, laughing.

"Linda was so excited," Jerry added. "She kept insisting we meet with you. She was adamant that we write down what we wanted to do in our desirement years and that we needed to get involved in our companies' 401(k) plans; '10–1–NOW!' she kept chanting."

We all laughed.

"Of course, her enthusiasm made me even more skeptical," Jerry remembered.

"Why was that?" I asked.

"What she was saying was so foreign to me. I always figured that if we both just kept working hard enough and paying our bills, everything would take care of itself. The mortgage would be paid off—eventually. One day the kids would head off to lead their own lives and we'd coast into retirement, start collecting our Social Security, and travel. It's what my parents did. My dad worked in the steel industry for forty years. When he retired, my mom and dad had their Social Security and his pension. Their house was paid off. And while they never had a ton of money, they didn't owe anybody anything."

"Yes, but they didn't do anything either," Linda added. "Your dad's health gave out when he was fifty-eight. He retired at fifty-nine so he could start collecting his pension, but they never went anywhere or did anything. They just sat at home."

"That's true," agreed Jerry.

"And the sad thing," continued Linda, "was that he died at sixty-three, just one year after he started collecting Social Security. So he worked his whole life and paid into a system that never paid him back."

"Well," I started, looking over Jerry and Linda's file, thick with notes and reports from our twenty years of working together, "you two definitely get the award for the couple who followed each and every one of my Paychecks for Life Principles."

I had logged on to their personal Paychecks for Life website, which we create for our clients, to aggregate their financial affairs, and I now brought up their current balance sheet.

Linda and Jerry's Balance Sheet, 2008

Assets		Liabilities	
Home	$450,000	Mortgage (nine years remaining)	$50,000
Savings	$50,000		
Desirement accounts:			
Jerry's PCM Co.	$399,733		
Linda's PCM Co.	$303,969		
Cars + miscellaneous	$37,000	Car loan (two years remaining)	$10,000
Total assets	**$1,240,702**	**Total liabilities**	**$60,000**

Net worth (assets–liabilities) = $1,180,702

The amounts for Jerry and Linda's Paycheck Manufacturing Companies (PCM Cos.) represent the total value of their desirement accounts, including their 401(k) plans and IRA accounts. After we met in 1988, they had both begun to contribute 10% of their salaries each year. In addition, they began taken advantage of Other People's Money—OPM—and received matching contributions of 3% of their income from their companies each year. As their incomes grew, so did the amount of their contributions, since they continued to invest 10% of their annual pay in their PCM Cos. By 1998, both of their children were out of college and out of the house. "Free at last!" Jerry sang. This gave them extra disposable income to increase their contributions even more. Jerry began maxing out his 401(k) contribution (which was $10,000 in 1998) each year and Linda increased her contribution to 15% of her annual income. In addition, they continued to receive their companies' matching contributions.

"I was just going to put the extra savings we gained from being empty nesters into the bank," Jerry reminisced, "until you convinced me to invest in our Paycheck Manufacturing Companies. Looking at our financials now, I'm sure glad we followed your advice, Coach."

"I'm glad we did too," Linda added, smiling at her husband as she held his hand.

Both had invested in a diversified portfolio and taken advantage of dollar cost averaging and annual rebalancing.

"Not bad," Jerry smiled as he examined the balance sheet. "We're the millionaires next door you hear people talk about. This is certainly a far cry from where we were when we first met you twenty years ago."

It was true; the investments they had made in their PCM Cos., compounded for twenty years, had indeed made them the millionaires next door.

To show them the progress they had made since our first meeting, I pulled up their balance sheet from 1988.

Linda and Jerry's Balance Sheet, 1988

Assets		Liabilities	
Home	$300,000	Mortgage	$250,000
Savings	$5,000	Credit Card Debt	$15,000
Desirement accounts:	$0		
Cars + miscellaneous	$22,000	Car loan	$20,000
Total assets	**$327,000**	**Total liabilities**	**$285,000**
Net worth (assets–liabilities) = $42,000			

"Pretty bleak," Jerry commented. "I'm surprised you even took us on as clients."

"I was desperate," I joked. We all laughed.

Next, I pulled out a statement that showed the projected balances of their desirement accounts in five years and their expected paychecks for life (see page 16). The projection assumed they'd continue to invest in a diversified target date fund and use dollar cost averaging and annual rebalancing, and that the return on their investments would average 7% per year.

Linda and Jerry's Projected Desirement Account Balances and Annual Paychecks for Life

	Age	Projected desirement account balance	Projected annual paychecks for life
Jerry	65	$780,135	$38,000
Linda	60	$582,333	$28,000
Total		**$1,362,468**	**$66,000**

"Wow!" Jerry exclaimed. "Those last five years really make a big difference in the growth of our PCM Cos."

"Yes," I explained. "Remember Principle #4 about compound interest, one of the most powerful forces in the universe. It works magic in your later years."

The numbers were impressive, especially considering that in 2008, Jerry's income was $80,000 and Linda's was $50,000, for a total of $130,000. The table shows projected desirement account balances of $780,135 for Jerry and $582,333 for Linda, a total of $1,362,468. At age sixty-five, Jerry will start receiving an annual paycheck of $38,000, while Linda will take in $28,000 at age sixty, for a total annual paycheck of $66,000 (assuming they draw out 5% of their projected balances).

"Wow, I can actually retire at age sixty," Linda marveled.

"And we can live out our desirement years doing everything we've always wanted to do," Jerry smiled, his arms crossed in a relaxed fashion over his head.

Paychecks for Life

I pulled up yet another statement showing that Linda and Jerry's total annual paychecks for life, including Social Security payments, would be $96,000 per year—equal to 74% of their 2008 working income.

Linda's and Jerry's Total Annual Paychecks for Life, Including Social Security

	Guaranteed paychecks (Social Security)	Variable paychecks (401(k) plans)	Total annual paychecks for life
Jerry	$18,000	$38,000	$56,000
Linda	$12,000	$28,000	$40,000
Total	**$30,000**	**$66,000**	**$96,000**

I looked over at Jerry and Linda, who were holding hands and smiling at each other. A sense of contentment permeated the room. They realized that in just six short years they'd have 74% of their current earned income waiting for them in the form of their PCM Cos. In the middle of one of the worst financial crises since the Great Depression, the couple was unscathed by the turmoil in the global markets, secure in the knowledge that their PCM Cos. were successfully humming along.

What was it that gave Jerry and Linda the complete confidence that nothing would shatter their dreams of having paychecks for life by the time they reached their desirement years? What guarantee did they have that this would happen, given the bleak economic environment in 2008?

What this couple did, 20 years ago, was make a commitment to their financial future. This commitment required that they save a percentage of their paychecks every month for thirty years, through good and bad financial times. It also required them to commit to my nine Paychecks for Life Principles. To learn how they did this, just turn the page.

America's Savings Plan

The 401(k)

While it sounds like a lost cousin to the *Star Wars* characters R2-D2 and C-3PO, the 401(k) is simply an individual savings plan offered to employees of many corporations, thanks to some unintended provisions in the tax laws. Just like many bureaucratic innovations ranging from license plates to tax forms, the 401(k) name appears to be crafted from a meaningless series of letters and numbers.

The basic idea behind the 401(k) is that it allows employees to put a portion of their current income, called the contribution, into several investments on a pre-tax basis. That is, contributions are not subject to federal or state taxes (in most states); instead, these taxes are deferred until the time of withdrawal. (Contributions are, however, subject to Social Security and Medicare taxes.)

While the roots of the 401(k) plan were established through government regulation, the government didn't intend it to be an employee retirement plan. In 1978, Congress amended the *Revenue Act* to include a provision—Sec. 401(k), for which the plans are named—whereby employees were not to be taxed on income they chose to receive as deferred compensation rather than direct cash payments. The law went into effect on January 1, 1980.

That year, a tax consultant named Ted Benna was revamping a bank's retirement program. The bank was looking for a tax break and a way to gain an edge over its competitors. In particular, it wanted to replace its annual cash bonus plan with a deferred profit-sharing plan. This type of plan would allow it to contribute a portion of profits each year to a trust fund, invested at its discretion, that would pay money to employees upon their retirement.

Benna felt that the newly created 401(k) provision might be the key to the deferred profit-sharing plan his client was looking for. He suggested that employees could contribute some or all of their tax-deferred cash bonuses into a so-called 401(k) plan. He also thought of adding a matching employer contribution. Large employers already offered employee saving plans with pre-tax dollars, but up until this time, employees were not able to contribute their money on a pre-tax basis. Benna realized it would be possible to change those plans so that employees would be able to put their money in before rather than after tax. Rather than employers paying the bonuses and giving workers the choice to defer, he thought, why not let employees defer part of their own salary, pre-tax, and get an employer to match funds as an incentive?

Ironically, attorneys for Benna's client bank rejected the idea. They were afraid something so revolutionary would be challenged by the Internal Revenue Service (IRS). As a result, the first 401(k) plan was developed for Benna's own employer, The Johnson Companies. On January 1, 1981, the IRS officially sanctioned pre-tax salary reductions, and the 401(k) savings plan revolution began. Today, 401(k) assets are estimated at $4.5 trillion.

Next to your home, your 401(k) probably represents the second largest asset you'll own in your lifetime. Converting your home into a paycheck for life will hardly be an option, since you'll always need a place to live. But converting your 401(k) into a Paycheck Manufacturing Company *is* an option, and that is what this book is about. The nine principles of the Paychecks for Life system will show you how easy it is.

The Paychecks for Life System

Nine Principles for Creating Paychecks for Life

Principle #1

Act Like an Entrepreneur

In 1931, writer James Truslow Adams coined the term "American Dream" in his book *The Epic of America*. While most Americans associate the term with home ownership, according to Truslow, it's much more than that. The American Dream is an extension of the Declaration of Independence, which states that all men are created equal; Truslow's use meant that dream of a land in which life should be better and richer and fuller for everyone, with opportunity for each according to ability or achievement.

While that's an illustrious ideal, it all hinges on a single word: opportunity. The American Dream is not a belief that everyone is simply handed big homes, fancy lifestyles, and better educations. Instead, it's a belief that everyone has an equal opportunity to obtain them.

You have the opportunity for a richer, fuller American Dream by securing your retirement years. Don't expect the government to hand a secure future to you in the form of Social Security. You must create it. You must build your very own Paycheck Manufacturing Company (PCM Co.). You must become your own boss. You must become an entrepreneur.

According to the dictionary, an entrepreneur is:

- one who organizes, manages, and assumes the risks of a business or enterprise;
- one who takes land, labor, and capital and combines them in such a way that more value is created than the cost to obtain those resources;
- one whose final product is worth more than the sum of its individual parts.

To these definitions, I would add:

- one who figures out what products or services are needed and then finds the people (talent) who can make the idea become a reality, all the while spending less money than will be received. In other words, one who recognizes opportunities and seizes them.

For example, a baker buys relatively cheap flour, butter, spices, and other ingredients. By using his or her expertise and creativity, those simple parts can be mixed, baked, and shaped into a glamorous wedding cake worth thousands of dollars. The baker takes ingredients from a lower level of productivity, and by adding his talent, brings them to a higher level of productivity (and profitability) in the form of the expensive wedding cake.

At the moment, you're an employee acting as a resource for an entrepreneur, the person who owns the company for which you work. That person, your boss, is using your skills and taking them from a lower level of productivity to a higher one, consequently creating more value than the money he or she has invested. When I ask entrepreneurs like your boss, "What's your retirement plan?" they unanimously answer, "Charlie, you're sitting in it!" Every day, your boss dreams about the time when he or she will sell the business and sail off into the sunset with paychecks for life. All of this excess value is not being created for nothing; your boss is doing it to reap the benefits, so he or she has a big incentive to make sure resources are used fully and efficiently to maximize those benefits. You need to do the same thing.

Now I know what you're thinking: "What are you talking about, Charlie? I've worked my entire life for someone else and probably will continue to do so until the day I retire."

That last part is true—you probably will continue to have an employer throughout your working life; however, you still have the ability to build a business inside the one you work for. Best of all, both your employer and the U.S. government want you to do this and will even invest in your business.

So what kind of business am I talking about?

As we have already learned, the government and your employer call it your 401(k) plan. Like the majority of American workers, you probably believe your company 401(k) plan is your employer's, not yours. It's something they have established, and you have nothing to do with it. It's just this kind of thinking that will cause you to miss the opportunity to create, invest in, and build a business that you, too, can sell someday and turn into paychecks for life.

> *"Like the majority of American workers, you probably believe your company 401(k) plan is your employer's, not yours."*

Your Paycheck Manufacturing Company

To be an entrepreneur, you must act like one. That means you must be prepared to accept a higher level of responsibility. You must weigh all decisions carefully. You must be thorough, efficient and cautious.

So how do you get started? Well, the first step is the easiest. Give your company's 401(k) plan a name. Use your own name or just make something up. Call it your _____(fill in the blank) Paycheck Manufacturing Company (PCM Co.).

Oh yes, assume you just incorporated it, so put today's date after the name so you'll always remember the day you founded your business:

_____ PCM Co., incorporated _____.
Company Name   mm/dd/yyyy

By taking the decisive action of naming your 401(k) PCM Co., you begin a very important process: taking ownership of and responsibility for your financial future. The act of naming something as an owner shifts you from being under the control of that thing to being in charge of it. When you're in charge of something you're 100% responsible for the end result. No more pointing the finger and blaming others for the operation and success of your PCM Co. No more blaming the government or your current employer for what you don't have. The buck, as President Harry S. Truman once said, stops here, with you as boss. As the owner of your PCM Co., it's time to start acting and behaving like a successful entrepreneur who works every day to manage and build your enterprise, and truly believes the future is yours for the taking.

Contribution Dollars: The Best Employees in the World

To operate a successful business, you can't go it alone. You need employees.

> *"The dollars inside your 401(k) are the employees of your PCM Co., and they're the best employees imaginable: they work 24/7/365—twenty-four hours a day, seven days a week, 365 days a year."*

The dollars inside your 401(k) are the employees of your PCM Co., and they're the best employees imaginable: they work 24/7/365—twenty-four hours a day, seven days a week, 365 days a year. They work while you sleep and they never complain. You don't have to pay their health benefits, and you don't have to pay taxes on them today.

Your PCM Co. Employees

Knowing what you now know about these workers, if you could hire as many of them as you wanted, when would you hire them? As soon as you can! The sooner you do so, the sooner your PCM Co. will balloon with enough money to finance your own travels off into the sunset, just like the entrepreneur who owns the company you work for.

Here's another critical question: how many of these amazing employees should you bring into your PCM Co.? As many as you can! Unfortunately, too many people hire—contribute—only 2%, or 3%, or 6% of their income to work in their PCM Co. That's not enough. Once you understand that your 401(k) is really your very own PCM Co. and that you're its board chair and its CEO, you'll realize that you need to invest a significantly larger percentage of your pay each month. As of 2009, the government will allow you to hire up to $16,500 of these employee dollars—and if you're over the age of fifty, you can usually hire another $5,500. That's $22,000 of 24/7/365, hard-working, never-complaining, non-quitting, non-taxable, cost-free capital employees to work in your PCM Co. every year. Why not hire as close to the limit as you can, as soon as you can, and beat your boss to retirement? Why not start thinking and winning like an entrepreneur who invests dollars, time, and energy in the success of his or her company? You must.

I know what you might be saying right now: "Charlie, I have other bills to pay. I can't afford to hire (invest) that much money." Well, as you'll see with the nine Paychecks for Life principles, it's extremely important that you begin investing even a small percentage of your current income—1%, 2%, even 3%—and put the power of marginal thinking to work for you today.

The Power of Marginal Thinking

Entrepreneurs are masters at thinking in small increments. In the field of financial economics, this is called "marginal thinking," and it is the foundation for solving big, complex problems by answering small, easy questions.

> *"To make a decision—any decision—you must always compare the benefits gained with the costs."*

Believe it or not, you use this technique all the time to solve problems—you just don't refer to it as marginal thinking. You may even be unaware that you're using it, but you are. To make a decision—any decision—you must always compare the benefits gained with the costs. If the benefits are greater than or equal to the costs, you accept the action. If not, you reject it. It's that simple.

The Pizza Quiz

For example, assume you want to have pizza for lunch and that it costs $3.00 per slice. How many should you order? That's actually a difficult question if you had to pinpoint the exact amount the moment you enter the restaurant. Instead, begin by asking how much one slice is worth to you now. If you're really hungry, you may be willing to pay $5.00 per slice. That's the value to you. Because it will cost only $3.00, you order your first slice and, of course, gain some satisfaction from it. You're not quite as hungry as when you entered the restaurant.

The Pizza Quiz

What's another slice worth to you now? Because you're not as hungry, a second slice may be worth $4.00 to you. You can buy another slice for only $3.00, so once again, the benefit to you is greater than the cost to obtain it. You decide to buy the second slice.

After finishing the second slice, you're even less hungry than after the first. Each additional slice diminishes your hunger a little bit, thereby causing the next slice to provide less satisfaction. In other words, each additional slice has less value to you. This is important to understand. The more you consume of something, the less value each additional unit has.

Perhaps you're willing to pay $3.00 for a third slice; since that's exactly what the store charges, you go ahead and place your order.

The process continues until, eventually, you reach a point where you feel there's no additional benefit from eating one more slice. At that point, you stop. If you'd be willing to pay only $2.00 for a fourth slice, you'd stop after three—you would not pay $3.00 in exchange for something worth only $2.00 to you. You're better off without it.

As this example shows, the complex problem of determining exactly how much to eat was easily solved in increments. It was solved by marginal thinking.

Let's assume you also decided on a soft drink to go with your pizza. A 12-oz drink is $2.00 and a 16-oz drink is $2.25. The question is not whether you should have a drink. You've already decided that. The question is how much it's worth, which is solved by marginal thinking. Is it worth paying an additional twenty-five cents for another four ounces? If the answer is yes, take the sixteen ounces. If not, stay with the small.

Marginal thinking can be used to solve problems even when there's not an explicit cost in dollars and cents. For instance, should you hit the snooze control on your alarm clock in the morning? By silencing the annoying alarm, there's a benefit to you (more sleep) but there's also a cost (less time to get ready for work). Each time you hit the snooze control, you get additional sleep. However, the more sleep you get, the less value additional sleep will have. Eventually the cost to you will be greater than the benefit (the costs of rushing for work, skipping breakfast, speeding down the highway, and so forth are not worth the additional ten minutes of silence offered by the snooze control). At that point, it's time to get up.

Now that you understand what marginal thinking is all about, you'll notice it everywhere. How many hours should I work? How much education should I attain? How many minutes do I need on my cell phone plan? How much gas should I pump in my car? And, of course, how much or how long should I invest in my PCM Co.? All of these seemingly complex questions are easily answered by marginal thinking.

If You Want to Get Big, Think Small

Let's assume you're trying to decide how much to contribute to your PCM Co. As with the pizza example, that's a difficult decision; however, what if I told you that a 5% contribution has an expected value of $500,000 when you retire, but 6% has an expected value of $650,000? Is it worth it to you to increase from 5% to 6%? Can you now appreciate how easy the answers are with marginal thinking? When you break complex problems into small bites—marginal bites—the answers are clear.

Here are some other examples: What if you can expect to have $100,000 at retirement by taking zero risk in your 401(k), but that you can increase that to $500,000 by taking only slightly more risk? Would you do it? Or what if you could reduce the expenses to operate your 401(k) by just 0.50% and thereby generate $200,000 more when you retire? Would you do what's necessary to make this marginal change? What if you could expect to receive $500,000 at retirement by starting your PCM Co. in five years, but could expect three times that by starting today? Would you start immediately?

We could continue this line of questioning until your answer is no. At that point, we've determined the amount of risk or the type of actions you should take in your PCM Co. Marginal thinking provides the method for making those critical decisions in your PCM Co. My nine Paychecks for Life Principles, starting with this one, are all about marginal thinking. Put them all together and you have a formula for exponential results that will generate paychecks for life and create financial independence with reduced financial anxiety.

PAYCHECKS FOR LIFE ACTION STEPS

☐ Entrepreneurs focus every day on successfully managing their businesses because they dream someday of selling those businesses and sailing happily off into the sunset with paychecks for life from the sale. You need to do the same.

☐ Begin thinking of your 401(k) as your very own Paycheck Manufacturing Company (PCM Co.). The first step is to name it: _____ PMC Co., incorporated _____ (today's date). Why? The act of naming something is the act of taking ownership.

☐ The dollars you invest in your PCM Co. are like the employees your boss hires to work in his or her company, only better. Your employees work 24/7/365 and never complain. Hire as many as you can as fast as you can.

☐ To act like an entrepreneur, you must practice marginal thinking. Always think and act in small increments. The results will be exponential.

☐ Think of the money you contribute each pay period to your 401(k) as an investment in your PCM Co. and your ability to receive paychecks for life.

Principle #2

Determine Your Desirement Mortgage

Did you know that one of the dictionary definitions of retirement is "to put out of use"? Think about that. Is that what you're working for—to be put out of use when you retire? I doubt it. I don't know of anyone who dreams throughout their working days of being put out to pasture at age sixty-five or seventy. Instead of using the words "retirement years," I am choosing to call these years your "desirement years." Doesn't that sound better? These are the years you will get to enjoy when you stop working in your current occupation and devote yourself to all the things you've been dreaming about doing some day.

If there's one thing I know from speaking to thousands of working people just like you, it's that not a single working day goes by in which you don't think about what you'd rather be doing than working, even if you love your job. It's human nature to dream about all those things you would do with your time if you didn't have to work. All the things you want to do are what I call your desirements.

The Three Phases of Investing

When it comes to personal finances, I think of life as having three distinct stages, as shown below.

The Three Phases of Investing

Earning years	Squirreling years	Desirement years
Accumulate	Protect	Spend
Ages 21 to 54	Ages 55 to 64	Ages 65 to life expectancy

Earning Years

Your primary earning years usually last from ages twenty-one to fifty-four (though they may start earlier or go later depending on when you choose to start or stop working). These are the years when you need to accumulate money in your PCM Co. The sooner you start, the sooner compound interest will go to work for you (see Principle #4 starting on page 67). Remember that the dollars you invest are your PCM Co.'s employees. They're ready to work for you 24/7/365, through good markets and bad, with one purpose: to create your paychecks for life.

Squirreling Years

From ages fifty-five to sixty-four, you should protect an increasing percentage of your capital from the effects of investment bear markets that might occur at the beginning of your desirement years. You want to reduce your exposure to riskier investments in your 401(k) and move into safer havens like bonds or cash equivalents.

The key thing to understand here is that a bear market can last three to six years and can represent a loss of 20% or more to the value of your PCM Co. To protect this value, you should move an increasing percentage of your money into more conservative bonds and cash equivalents when you are between ages fifty-five and sixty-four, until you have accumulated enough reserve money to cover the cost of three to five years of your income needs in your desirement years.

Desirement Years

At this stage, your investment strategy should be to protect your hard-earned capital and generate income. Your goal is to earn a needs-based rate of return equal to or slightly higher than taxes and inflation, which should be a very conservative 5% to 7%.

The Entrepreneurial Spirit

In the previous chapter, I said you need to think like an entrepreneur if you're to maximize your PCM Co. Entrepreneurs have a deep-seated belief that their future is bigger than their past. They consistently plan and dream about what the future can and will look like. They believe wholeheartedly that if they set specific goals, actually write them down, and fine-tune them on a weekly, monthly, quarterly, and annual basis, that they'll be successful in creating a future that's much more fulfilling than their past. This is the entrepreneurial spirit, and you must embrace it fully.

Now I know what you might be thinking. "What, me? I can't do that, Charlie! Do you have any idea what my circumstances are? My income is not that high, I hate my job, and I have too much debt."

My answer to that is that we all have specific circumstances in our lives that might seem like barriers to our aspirations; focusing solely on these will certainly limit our ability to be more successful and achieve our dreams. I believe that if you let your past dictate your future, you certainly will end up right where you are now. To stop that from happening, you have to start writing down your dreams and goals for your desirement years.

The Desirement Planning Process

"You have to believe that your future is bigger than your past."

You have to believe your future is greater than your past, that what lies ahead is bigger and better. The desirement planning process is your first step toward securing your financial future with reduced anxiety. The process involves two critical steps for calculating what the cost of your retirement (desirement) years will be and for creating a financial mechanism for covering these costs long after your paychecks have stopped.

Step One: Create Your Desirement Wish List

In a moment, I am going to ask you to close your eyes and imagine all of the things you've dreamed about doing some day, when you're no longer working. Imagine the exotic places you've always wanted to visit, the second home you'd love to build or buy, that cruise you've always wanted to take to some exotic island, those recreational activities—sailing, fishing, hunting, skiing, mountain climbing, hiking, parachuting—you've long desired to try. Perhaps you want to go back to school or teach, become active in charities that could use your help, plant the garden you've always wanted, renovate the house, read all the books you've been keeping on a list, or just spend more time with your grandchildren. The possibilities are endless.

Now close your eyes and let your imagination run wild. Come on! Just play along with me and close your eyes. After all, it's your brighter future I'm talking about, and you will add to your Desirement Wish List throughout your working years! It represents your desirements and what you'll do in your retirement years. In the appendix, there's a blank Desirement Wish List you can complete.

Step Two: Calculate Your Desirement Mortgage Number

The next step is to put a price tag on all the wonderful things you want to do and have in your desirement years. These can be broken down into:

1. Fixed expenses, such as your house costs, taxes, and utilities
2. Desirement costs, such as experiences, possessions, achievements

The Personal Desirement Paycheck Analysis worksheet will help you calculate these costs (refer to Appendix).

I know what you're thinking. "This is complicated, Charlie. I can barely calculate and budget my current expenses. How do you expect me to figure out what something is going to cost me twenty, thirty or possibly forty years from now?"

You're right—it's a difficult task. So I've made it easier. All you need to calculate is your desirement number, which represents the sum total of the money you'll need to create a paycheck for life that will cover all those things you want to do and will do in your desirement years. You can calculate your desirement number by using the "income replacement" approach and my Desirement Mortgage Calculator.

Your income replacement figure

A simple way to calculate how much money you'll need to pay for all the things on your Desirement Wish List is to assume you'll need 70, 80 or 90% of your current income, adjusted for inflation, in your desirement years to maintain your current lifestyle. Of course, if your wish list contains things that will cost a lot more than your current lifestyle, you'll need to factor these costs into your future income need. This approach assumes your children have moved out and are not an ongoing expense, and that your home mortgage is paid off, so you don't need 100% of your current income to maintain your lifestyle in your desirement years.

As an example, let's say you're thirty-five years old, that your current income is $40,000, and that you want to retire by age sixty-five. If you think you'll only need 70% of your current income in your desirement years, than you'd need $28,000 starting at age sixty-five.

This income replacement figure of $28,000 must be adjusted for inflation, since the cost of living continues to go up, not down. Inflation silently erodes the future purchasing power of your money as costs continue to rise for food, gas, health care, travel, and so on. In other words, a $28,000 income thirty years from now is not going to buy $28,000 worth of goods and services. If inflation averages 3% for thirty years, you'll need an income of $67,963 a year starting at age sixty-five to keep pace with inflation.

Your lump sum desirement number

The following table shows how this thirty-five-year-old's income would grow keeping pace with 3% cost-of-living adjustments (also known as inflation).

Income Growth Accumulation Years

Accumulation Years		
Year	Salary	Balance
35	$40,000	$0
36	$41,200	$15,263
37	$42,436	$31,467
38	$43,709	$48,670
39	$45,020	$66,935
40	$46,371	$86,326
41	$47,762	$106,913
42	$49,195	$128,770
43	$50,671	$151,975
44	$52,191	$176,611
45	$53,757	$202,766
46	$55,369	$230,535
47	$57,030	$260,017
48	$58,741	$291,317
49	$60,504	$324,547
50	$62,319	$359,827
51	$64,188	$397,283
52	$66,114	$437,050
53	$68,097	$497,269
54	$70,140	$524,092
55	$72,244	$571,679
56	$74,412	$622,202
57	$76,644	$675,840
58	$78,934	$732,787
59	$81,312	$793,247
60	$83,751	$857,435
61	$86,264	$925,583
62	$88,852	$997,933
63	$91,517	$1,074,746
64	$94,263	$1,156,297

By age sixty-four, this thirty-five-year-old's $40,000 income would have grown to $94,263. In other words, to purchase the same goods and services thirty years from now, his income would have had to grow to $94,263.

The next table shows that if we assume he will only need 70% of his $40,000 income adjusted for inflation by age sixty-five, than he needs $67,963 a year to live on.

But wait! Inflation doesn't stop when you enter your desirement years; it continues to erode the value of your hard-earned dollars. As you can see in the following table, to maintain his 70% lifestyle, our example earner's income needs continue to grow by 3% inflation. By the time he's eighty, he needs $105,885. And by his life expectancy of eighty-six, he needs $126,432.

Income Growth Distribution Years

| | Distribution Years | |
Year	Need	Balance
65	$67,963	$1,209,652
66	$70,002	$1,212,106
67	$72,102	$1,212,546
68	$74,265	$1,210,784
69	$76,493	$1,206,616
70	$78,788	$1,199,826
71	$81,152	$1,190,181
72	$83,586	$1,177,432
73	$86,094	$1,161,312
74	$88,677	$1,141,535
75	$91,337	$1,117,796
76	$94,077	$1,089,769
77	$96,899	$1,057,104
78	$99,806	$1,019,428
79	$102,801	$976,341
80	$105,885	$927,419
81	$109,061	$872,204
82	$112,333	$810,212
83	$115,703	$740,923
84	$119,174	$663,782
85	$122,749	$578,198
86	$126,432	$483,540
87	$130,225	$379,134
88	$134,132	$264,261
89	$138,155	$138,155

As you can see in the column marked Balance, our thirty-five-year-old will need $1,209,652 to generate his paycheck for life.

Your first reaction may be, "Are you crazy, Charlie? There's no way I could possibly save that amount of money by myself." I agree. You can't do it on your own. But you can do it with your PCM Co.

Social Security

At the beginning of this book, I said your Social Security statement is really your eviction notice. The government is putting you on notice that there "may" not be any social security payments to look forward to.

No one knows for sure what's going to happen to Social Security. I believe the system will change to an income means testing program. In other words, the government will look at how much income you have and, based on a certain income level, not pay any benefits or pay reduced benefits. They might say that if you receive income over a certain level—let's say $75,000 to $100,000 from all sources, both earned and unearned—you don't really need Social Security and won't receive it. For the majority of median income earners in retirement, I believe the government will continue to provide Social Security benefits.

What this means is that a portion of your $1,209,652 savings need can be reduced by guaranteed income benefits you may receive from a pension plan, Social Security, or other deferred compensation source. But include Social Security only if you feel confident the government will not evict you from the system.

For the purposes of this exercise, let's assume that, starting at age sixty-five, Social Security will pay you $1,250 per month or $15,000 per year. The present value of the Social Security payments you would collect to your life expectancy (age eighty-six) is approximately $241,702.

Future value of current retirement assets (i.e. existing 401(k) plans or individual retirement accounts (IRAS))

Let's say you already have $45,000 invested in various retirement accounts (the average American has $42,000 saved for retirement). We can project the value of those assets at age sixty-five. There are a variety of compound interest calculators online, such as Money Chimp (www.moneychimp.com), that you can use to calculate the future value of an investment. Assuming you earn a conservative 6% on your money each year for the next thirty years, your $45,000 will be worth $271,015. A tidy sum.

Your Desirement Mortgage number

We can now calculate your Desirement Mortgage number.

First, what do I mean by a Desirement Mortgage? Earlier in the book, I told you that the two largest assets you will ever own are most likely your home and your 401(k) PCM Co. I'd like you to remember how you purchased your first home.

Your first home purchase

Think back to the time just before you bought the first home of your dreams. What did you do? You dreamt about it, and probably talked about it with your spouse or significant other every day. Then you started looking at houses, until one day, you found it. Remember what a great feeling that was and how excited you were? Remember how much you wanted that home, no matter the cost, even if it was just a little out of your budget? And what did you do if it was? You bought it anyway.

If you were like most first-time homebuyers you worried about how you were going to come up with the down payment for that home and then how you'd make the mortgage payment each month. And I'll bet that after you purchased that house and made some adjustments in your monthly budget, you found making the monthly mortgage payment wasn't so hard after all. You were able to make the payment no matter what, through good stock markets and bad, through one child to seven. It all worked out. Why?

It worked because you made a commitment to something you really wanted, something you desired, something you would own (and finance) for at least thirty years. You may have renovated your first home, or moved to a larger one. You've been paying a monthly mortgage for the past couple of decades.

What was it that helped you make the dream of home ownership a reality? Unconsciously, you had a formula for success that allowed you to achieve your dream. The formula probably looked something like this:

Your Home Ownership Formula for Success

1. You identified your dream house and what it would cost.
2. You committed to paying for your dream house within a certain period of time.
3. You calculated what it would cost, i.e. what you could afford to finance each month as a mortgage payment.
4. You saved for your down payment.

41

5. You adjusted your plan and budget to overcome unforeseen financial obstacles that might prevent you from achieving your dream of home ownership.
6. You never stopped believing you could save for and finance your goal of home ownership.
7. You achieved your dream (desirement) and purchased your first home.

A home mortgage

And how did you go about purchasing that first home? Did you show up at the closing with bags of cash to pay for it? No. Instead, you made a small down payment, probably 10–20%, and financed the rest over a specific number of years (say, 15 to 30). In other words, you took out a home mortgage (one of the great financial instruments of the twentieth century). You used an installment plan to pay off your home on a monthly basis.

Let's say your first home cost $300,000 and that you put 20% (or $60,000) down. That left $240,000 for you to finance with a mortgage. Assuming you got a low, fixed mortgage rate of 6% for thirty years, how much was your monthly mortgage payment (excluding taxes and insurance)? Using a mortgage calculator like the one at www.moneychimp.com, we find your monthly payment would be $1,438.92. Over thirty years, these payments equal an investment of $518,012—more than double the original $240,000 you borrowed from the bank! (See figure below.) The total amount of interest you paid to the bank over thirty years is $278,012.

The True Cost of a Home Mortgage

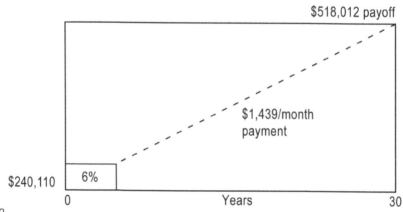

$518,012 payoff

$1,439/month payment

$240,110   6%

0   Years   30

Your Desirement Mortgage number

I now want you to think about your desirement number in exactly the same way as you thought of your first home. Let's imagine that the $1,209,652 desirement number (the amount of money a thirty-five-year old, retiring at age sixty-five, needs to generate a paycheck for life) is the cost of the home you want to buy. How can you finance this amount?

First you need a down payment. In this example, we're assuming you have two down payments:

1. Social Security, which is worth $241,702 and,
2. Retirement savings, which are worth $271,015 ($45,000 x 6% compounded monthly over 30 years)

The balance that you need to finance over 30 years is:

$$\$1,209,652 - (\$241,702 + \$271,015) = \$696,935$$

I want you to imagine that $696,935 is the cost of your first home. How would you go about purchasing it? Exactly! You would go to your local bank and take out a home mortgage of $696,935 for thirty years with a fixed mortgage rate.

In this case, since we're talking about financing your desirement years, the $696,935 is really your Desirement Mortgage number. Applying the same logic you used when financing your home with a mortgage, how much will you need to "pay" (save) each month to accumulate $696,935?

Using a compound interest calculator, we find you'll need to save approximately $8,280 a year, or $690 per month, assuming you earn 6% compounded monthly on your investment.

Your Desirement Mortgage

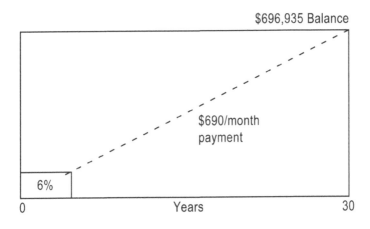

$696,935 Balance

$690/month
payment

6%

0   Years   30

I hope by now you're beginning to see the glaring similarities between a home mortgage and a Desirement Mortgage. Just as you had a formula for success for buying your first home (page 43), you can apply the same principles to successfully accumulating enough money in your PCM Co. to pay off your Desirement Mortgage.

Your Desirement Mortgage Formula for Success

1. You created your Desirement Wish List and calculated your desirement number.
3. You committed to funding your desirement years in a certain period of time. You calculated what it would cost each month to pay your desirement mortgage payment.
4. You calculated your down payment, i.e. what Social Security and any current retirement assets (401(k)s and IRAs) would be worth in your desirement years.
5. You adjusted your plan and budget to overcome unforeseen financial obstacles that might prevent you from achieving your dream of having a paycheck for life to fund your desirement years.
6. You never stopped believing you could save for and finance your goal of a financially secure desirement.
7. Congratulations! You have successfully funded your desirement mortgage and are generating paychecks for life in your desirement years.

The Desirement Mortgage Calculator

To make calculating your desirement number and Desirement Mortgage payment easier for you, I created the Desirement Mortgage Calculator. Go to www.paychecksforlife.org and click on Desirement Mortgage Calculator.

To summarize, I have used the following assumptions in Step 1: Find your Desirement Number:

1. Current age: 35
2. Desirement age: 65
3. Needs-based rate of return: 6%
4. Current annual income: $40,000
5. Annual raise (inflation): 3%

6. Annual Social Security income at retirement: $0
7. Desired percentage of income in retirement: 70% ($28,000 annually)

The desirement number is $1,209,652

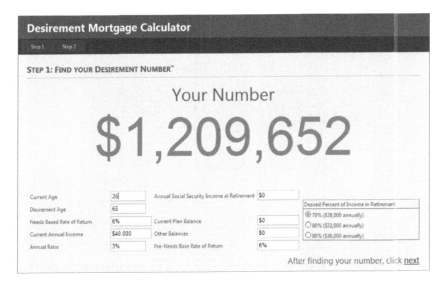

If we now use $15,000 in annual Social Security as part of the down payment, the desirement number is reduced to $967,950.

Existing retirement savings

If we also assume $45,000 in current retirement savings (current plan balance), the desirement number is reduced to $696,934.

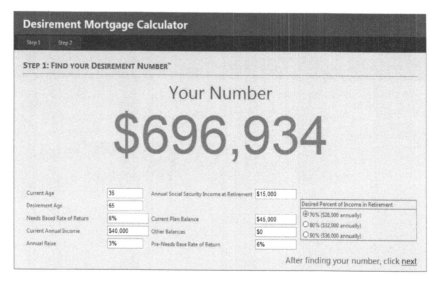

Try inputting your personal assumptions to calculate your desirement number and Desirement Mortgage monthly payment.

Needs-Based vs. Greeds-Based Rate of Return

One of the most important assumptions in these calculations is what I call your "needs-based rate of return." This is the return you must earn on your investments in your PCM Co. year in and year out to arrive at your desirement years with enough accumulated capital to generate systematic paychecks for life.

To get a better handle on what I mean by your needs-based rate of return, let me ask you a few questions. First, when you took out your home mortgage, did you want a high rate of interest from the bank, or a low rate? Obviously you wanted a low rate so your mortgage payment would be as low as possible.

Second, did you want a fixed mortgage rate or an adjustable? Again, the answer seems obvious: a fixed rate. Why? For certainty. This way you knew exactly how much your mortgage payment would be each month over the life of the mortgage.

All of this may seem incredibly obvious, except when we turn to how you manage the money you are about to invest in your PCM Co. to fund your desirement mortgage. If I asked you how much you want to earn on the investments in your 401(k), what would your answer be? Probably "as much as I can get, Charlie!" That answer is what I call your "greeds-based rate of return." It's what causes the average 401(k) investor to pick investments that have done well in the past, forgetting that historic performance is no guarantee of what will happen in the future. The greeds-based rate of return is what caused millions of 401(k) investors—perhaps you were one of them—to take undue risk with their investment choices and lose 40% or more of their value in 2008, and then blame their 401(k) for the results. The 401(k) wasn't to blame; investor greed and lack of proper management were. Your greeds-based rate of return is what causes you to treat your 401(k) plan like a casino rather than like your home.

The Country's Largest Casino

Let me ask you another question. Would you go to a casino, right now, and bet your house on "red number nine" at the roulette table? How about the craps table, "lucky seven?" Would you? Of course not. But that's exactly what you and millions of other Americans do every day when you attempt to pick the investments in your 401(k) plan without knowing your needs-based rate of return.

I can't begin in these pages to make you a savvy investor (as opposed to a crafty gambler), nor do I want to. What I can do is make you an intelligent entrepreneur and steward of the money in your PCM Co. by having you treat it with the same care and respect you do your home and home mortgage. If you do this, you'll arrive at your desirement years with two very secure assets: your home fully paid off and secure, and a 401(k) PCM Co. filled with enough dollars to generate paychecks for life.

You must remember that you're the owner and entrepreneur of your PCM Co. Before entrepreneurs invest in a business, they figure out the cost of raw materials, labor, overhead, and other expenses to bring their products or services from a lower level of productivity to a higher level so they can make the greatest profit with the least amount of risk. Before investing their money or someone else's, successful entrepreneurs know what their margin is and, more importantly, what they need to earn—their needs-based rate of return—on their investment to make a reasonable profit and maintain their lifestyle.

To be a successful entrepreneur and steward of your PCM Co., you must do the same. You must generate enough return on your money with the least amount of risk to generate paychecks for life throughout your desirement years. This means you must first calculate your needs-based rate of return before investing any money in your PCM Co. and resist investing for a greeds-based rate of return. Leave that kind of thrill for the money you take to the casino.

The Average Needs-Based Rate of Return: Your Risk-Free, Casino-Free Number

For the average worker today, their needs-based rate of return is between 5% to 7%. That's it. The exact rate depends on a number of variables, including the years you have until retirement, the amount of savings you currently have, and your desired amount of future income.

To put this 5% to 7% desirement mortgage rate in perspective, if you were to establish a simple cash balance pension plan today, which is a conservative retirement plan, you would have to hire an actuary to calculate how much money you would need to save to achieve a guaranteed amount of money at retirement. In making this calculation, the actuary would assume you could invest your money at a conservative rate of return of 5.1% to 5.5%.

Applying this pension-plan rate of return to your 401(k) essentially guarantees that your PCM Co. will accumulate enough funds to generate paychecks for life, and prevents you from gambling with your business. If you're still wondering why you'd want to do this, especially when you're staring at an investment option in your 401(k) that earned 40% last year, remember our discussion about how to be a successful entrepreneur and the power of marginal thinking. Great entrepreneurs do not assume a high margin (rate of return) that requires them to take undue risk that might cause them to lose their investment and eventually their business. You must make the same decisions and not be drawn in by the potential for high returns on investments you don't understand and can't afford to lose.

In the next chapter I'll show you how to use Other People's Money (OPM) in your PCM Co. and reduce your monthly desirement mortgage payment by 50% or more.

PAYCHECKS FOR LIFE ACTION STEPS

☐ To act like an entrepreneur, you must believe that your future is bigger than your past.

☐ Entrepreneurs set goals for themselves. They write them down and constantly revisit and adjust them. You must do the same with your goals for the future.

☐ Start by creating your desirement wish list.

☐ Next, determine your desirement mortgage. Calculate the future cost of both your fixed maintenance expenses and desirement expenses when you reach your desirement years, as well as the future value of your guaranteed and variable retirement assets.

☐ Begin to think about your desirement mortgage like you do your home mortgage. Both have the same characteristics: a down payment, monthly payments, a fixed rate of return, and a fixed term.

☐ Just like you did with your home mortgage, calculate the lowest fixed rate that will provide you with the amount you need to finance your desirement years. This is your needs-based rate of return, and it should be in the 5% to 7% range.

☐ Calculate the monthly payments you need to make to pay off your desirement mortgage.

☐ Go to www.paychecksforlife.org and use the Desirement Calculator to calculate your Desirement Mortgage Numbers.

Principle #3

Use Other People's Money to Capitalize Your Business

Even if you're new to investing and finance, you're probably familiar with the acronym OPM—Other People's Money. It's a common mantra in finance and even made for a great movie title starring Gregory Peck and Danny DeVito. On the more serious side, it was also the title of a collection of essays on the power of banks and financial institutions published in 1914 by Louis Brandeis, who later became one of the most influential members of the U.S. Supreme Court.

Whether used in a comedy movie or an essay to sway legal views, OPM combines two simple ideas: 1) It takes money to make money, and 2) If you don't have money, get it from other people. It's simple, but the effects are profound for your PCM Co.

All financial institutions capitalize on OPM. Banks lend it. Publicly traded companies borrow it. Mutual funds invest it. Of course, the government spends it. And then there's Bernie Madoff who simply stole it. The common thread is that all of them would rather risk your money than theirs. Without OPM, opportunities are limited. With OPM, opportunities exponentially increase.

> *"Without OPM, opportunities are limited. With OPM, opportunities exponentially increase."*

How Banks Use OPM: The Multiplier Effect

Take a bank, for instance. How does a bank make money? Most people never give this a second thought. They just assume that banks have a lot of money that they lend to others, but bankers are masters at using OPM and have taken it to a whole new level. They not only lend OPM, they lend money that doesn't even exist. How is that possible?

A bank attracts capital—OPM—by paying interest on cash balances. It then turns around and lends that cash to other people at higher interest rates. Simply put, banks take money from those who do not need it now (depositors) and transfers it to those who do (borrowers).

Remember one of our definitions of an entrepreneur: one who takes a resource—in this case OPM (capital)—and manipulates it in such a way that more value is created than the cost to obtain that resource. Banks act like entrepreneurs every day by maximizing the value of OPM.

Many people believe that 100% of their cash deposits are locked away tight in a personalized vault; the truth is that only a small fraction stays with the bank, and none of it stays in your account. Although funds are available if you should write a check or withdraw cash from an ATM machine, your deposits are immediately put to use in the bank's favor. If you do demand your money, the bank gets it, of course, from other people.

Banks are able to lend nearly all of people's deposits and shuffle funds from clients who do not immediately need the money to those who do because they operate on a fractional reserve system, which means they're required to keep only a fraction of deposits on reserve.

For each deposit made, only a small fraction, called the reserve require-ment, is held in the bank's vault. The balance becomes available for loans. The reserve requirement is set by the Federal Reserve and is usu-ally 10% or less. Although the requirement can be changed, it generally remains steady from year to year.

If you're starting to say, "Wait a minute, Charlie, this sounds like marginal (or fractional, in this case) thinking," then, by George, that entrepreneurial bug is starting to catch on.

Let's trace a simple bank deposit and see OPM in action. Assume you deposit $100 with a bank. The bank holds 10%, or $10, as the required reserve and lends the remaining $90 to another customer, who may deposit it with another bank. That bank, in turn, holds 10%, or $9.00, and lends the remaining $81. The process continues, but eventu-ally must stop since each back receives 10% less than the previous bank. Your initial $100 deposit has, therefore, created money that doesn't even exist. How much?

It turns out that if the reserve requirement is 10%, banks create an amount of money equal to one divided by the reserve requirement, or 1/0.10, which equals ten times the amount of printed money. Your $100 deposit is, therefore, expanded to $1,000. From a simple $100 deposit, $900 of additional money that never existed before is sud-denly created—for other people to borrow.

If it sounds like a potentially unstable system, you're right. That's exactly why many banks became insolvent during the 1930s when many "runs on the bank" occurred. If depositors believe that a bank is in financial trouble, they may all rush to the bank to withdraw their money, which, in turn, raises the risk of bank default, thus causing more people to withdraw money. A run on a bank is a psychological, self-perpetuating event. In other words, the banking system is stable as long as everyone believes that it is.

Today, many systems are in place to prevent such bank runs. There's the Federal Deposit Insurance Corporation (FDIC), which insures each depositor to $250,000 in the event of a bank failure. As long as you do not have more than $250,000 in cash deposited with the bank, you'd have no incentive to withdraw your money even if others are withdraw-ing theirs. The FDIC creates confidence for depositors. The greater the confidence, the less chance for bank failure.

There's also the Federal Reserve ("the Fed"), which acts as the "bankers' bank," ready, willing, and able to lend money to troubled banks in the event of bank panics. During the credit crisis of 2008, we witnessed the sheer leveraging power of the Federal Reserve. During one of the worst financial meltdowns since the Great Depression, the Fed created (printed) $700 billion in TARP (Troubled Asset Relief Program) funds, which it lent to the nation's largest banks to stimulate new bank lending and avoid a global run on the banking system. The more money in the banking system, the less chance of additional financial institution failure. Doing so restored confidence and faith in the financial system and markets.

So what's the point to understand from all of this? Banks make big money by taking OPM to another level—they lend money they don't even have. They have to do this to survive. Banks collect many short-term deposits but they make long-term loans, which creates a mismatch between their assets and liabilities. Without OPM, it's enormously difficult to invest efficiently. All forms of successful businesses, big and small, understand the importance of OPM. It's the only way they compete and survive.

> *"You, too, must make OPM part of your plan if you wish to create a steady stream of paychecks for life."*

You, too, must make OPM part of your plan if you wish to create a steady stream of paychecks for life. Without OPM, you'd have to invest your own money and earn all of the invested funds yourself. It would be a slow process. Don't forget that the employees of your PCM Co. are the dollars you invest. You need as many as you can get to work for you 24/7/365. Think how much faster your business will grow if you have access to OPM?

"But," you ask, "who are the other people who will give me money?" You actually have two partners in your PCM Co. who are willing and able to invest capital—OPM—into your business: Uncle Sam and your employer.

Your Business Partners

Partner #1: Uncle Sam's Money (USM)

Right now, take a one-dollar bill out of your wallet and hold it up in front of you. If you're in a 25% tax bracket and this was the last dollar in your paycheck, Uncle Sam would have taken twenty-five cents of that dollar. Go ahead, tear away 25% to see how it feels and what it looks like.

Uncle Sam's Take

Now let me ask you, what does Uncle Sam do with that twenty-five cents? He builds bridges and schools, manufactures airplanes and guns, provides agricultural programs, funds Medicaid, and so on—whatever he wants. Does he ever plan on giving it back to you once he's taken it? No.

Perhaps you're thinking, "Twenty-five cents of each dollar . . . what's the problem, Coach?"

Well, the problem isn't that you've just lost the twenty-five cents, never to be seen again. The problem is you have also lost the interest you could have earned on that quarter. Still doesn't sound like a lot?

Then let me ask you this question: if I gave you one penny of that twenty-five cents and you could double that penny every day for thirty days, how much would that be worth?

Ready for the answer?

$5,368,709.12

That's right: one penny compounded every day for a month equals $5,368,709.12.

We'll learn more about the power of compound interest in Principle #4, but for now I want you to understand that Uncle Sam is giving you a choice: either invest 100% of your dollar in your PCM Co., or give him a quarter and put seventy-five cents in your pocket to spend.

Guaranteed 33% return

Let's look at it another way. Let's assume you earn $100 and are in the 25% tax bracket. You can pay your taxes and take $75 home to spend. On the other hand, if you decide to invest the $100 in your 401(k), you're not taxed on that money—at least not yet. You'll be taxed when you eventually withdraw the funds, but the point is that the entire $100 contribution to your PCM Co. will begin working for you today. By choosing to invest in your 401(k), you have an additional $25 that was not available to you had you chosen to take the $75 on an after-tax basis.

That extra $25 was Uncle Sam's Money: USM. Those extra dollars—or put another way, those twenty-five extra employees working for you—represent a guaranteed 33% return on the money you have available to invest ($25 / $75). That alone should get your attention.

Interest-free loan

Another way to look at USM is that it really is an interest-free loan. Where else can you get a guaranteed 33% return on your money? Your local bank? Hardly. In 2010, interest rates on certificates of deposit were a miserly 1% to 2%.

As a successful entrepreneur, which you're becoming with each turn of the page of this book, you're always looking for OPM that you can borrow at the lowest rate possible. Well, USM is interest free!

I know what you're thinking: "What's the catch? What's my obligation for this interest-free USM?"

There are only two conditions. One, you must keep the money working in your PCM Co. until you're fifty-nine-and-a-half years old, at which point you can begin withdrawing funds without a 10% early withdrawal penalty. While you're not required to pay any interest on the use of this money until then, you'll be required to pay taxes when you withdraw it to generate your paychecks for life. The taxes you pay will be based on the prevailing tax rates during your desirement years.

Second, when you reach the age of seventy-and-a-half, Uncle Sam requires that you begin withdrawing a minimum amount from your PCM Co. each year. Why? Because Uncle Sam wants to begin getting repaid for the money he has allowed you to use, interest-free, all those years. In essence, USM is a demand note or IOU that starts to become due at age seventy-and-a-half at the latest. Your CPA or financial advisor can assist you in making that calculation each year.

Let me give you a word of caution. Many people believe that when they reach their desirement years they'll be in a lower tax bracket because their income will be lower. Let me put this myth to rest. The truth is that no one knows what tax bracket you'll be in when you stop working, including the government. You could actually be in a higher tax bracket than you are now.

"No one knows what tax bracket you'll be in when you stop working, including the government. You could actually be in a higher tax bracket than you are now."

Your 401(k) stimulus package

In my seminars, I often refer to the benefits of USM as a 401(k) stimulus package. Just as the government has thrown money at banks and other troubled businesses to bail them out of financial difficulty, it's giving you a similar opportunity. Why? One reason is the looming failure of Social Security. Providing access to an interest-free loan is a government incentive for you to secure your own well-being. Think like an entrepreneur and use this loan to stimulate your financial future today.

Partner #2: Your Employer's Money (YEM)

Your employer may also want to invest capital in your PCM Co. The government calls this investment a profit-sharing contribution, matching contribution or safe harbor contribution. The bottom line is, if your 401(k) plan has an employer contribution, then your employer is saying: "I want to invest in your PCM Co."

> *"The bottom line is, if your 401(k) plan has an employer contribution, then your employer is saying: 'I want to invest in your PCM Co.'"*

Let's assume that your employer matches the first 4% of the income that you contribute. What this means is that you earn a 100% return on that 4%—instantly. That's a remarkable return considering that the risk-free interest rate today is less than 1% per year and that the largest publicly traded corporations are proud to report a 20% return on assets at their annual shareholder meetings.

Your Employer's Money (YEM) generates a consistent return of up to 100% on some of your investment dollars, and it's risk free and interest free. Use it.

Vesting

Depending on the design of your current employer's 401(k) plan, the matching contribution is either automatically yours—which is known as 100% vested—or, more typically, will become yours beginning with 0% in the first year and then in increments of 20% per year over the next five years. At the end of six years all of the money your employer has invested in your PCM Co. remains inside your business (your 401(k)) even if you leave that place of employment.

The USM/YEM Multiplier Effect

Now let's look at the power of USM and YEM combined. Let's assume your employer will match half of the first 6% of the income you contribute to your PCM Co. This means on the first 6% of your pay, your employer will match 3%. Let's also assume you're in a 25% federal tax bracket.

Suppose 6% of your pay equals $100 and you decide to contribute this full amount into your PCM Co. Uncle Sam has actually lent you, interest free, $25 of this amount, so you have invested $75 of your own money and $25 of USM. Your employer, who is another partner in your PCM Co., will match 50% of your contribution, or $50. You now have $150 working in your PCM Co. instead of $75 in your pocket to spend. You have immediately doubled your money without even putting it into any investment. This is a risk-free rate you'll never find anywhere else. The higher your tax bracket, the more valuable the effect of USM and YEM.

The table on the following page shows the power of OPM over time. In the table I've made the following assumptions:

- Your annual income is $40,000.
- Your 401(k) savings rate is 10%.
- Your tax rate is 25%.
- Your employer matches 50% of your contribution up to the first 6% of your earnings.
- Your average rate of return is 7%.

OPM Calculator

Year	Annual Savings (After Tax)	Uncle Sam Money	Employer Match	Annual Total Invested	Prior Year Earnings	Balance	Total Saved	Return
1	$3,000.00	$1,000.00	$1,200.00	$5,200.00	$0.00	$5,200.00	$3,000.00	73%
5	$3,000.00	$1,000.00	$1,200.00	$5,200.00	$1,616.14	$29,903.84	$15,000.00	99%
10	$3,000.00	$1,000.00	$1,200.00	$5,200.00	$4,359.99	$71,845.53	$30,000.00	139%
15	$3,000.00	$1,000.00	$1,200.00	$5,200.00	$8,208.38	$130,670.91	$45,000.00	190%
20	$3,000.00	$1,000.00	$1,200.00	$5,200.00	$13,605.94	$213,176.56	$60,000.00	255%
25	$3,000.00	$1,000.00	$1,200.00	$5,200.00	$21,176.31	$328,895.00	$75,000.00	339%
30	$3,000.00	$1,000.00	$1,200.00	$5,200.00	$31,794.14	$491,196.09	$90,000.00	446%
35	$3,000.00	$1,000.00	$1,200.00	$5,200.00	$46,686.19	$718,831.77	$105,000.00	585%
40	$3,000.00	$1,000.00	$1,200.00	$5,200.00	$67,573.07	$1,038,102.58	$120,000.00	765%
45	$3,000.00	$1,000.00	$1,200.00	$5,200.00	$96,867.99	$1,485,896.42	$135,000.00	1001%
50	$3,000.00	$1,000.00	$1,200.00	$5,200.00	$137,955.64	$2,113,950.43	$150,000.00	1309%

Total Saved column equals the total Annual Savings less OPM (Uncle Sam's Money plus Employer Match)

A 401(k) savings rate of 10% on $40,000 is $4,000 per year. At a 25% tax rate, this means you have deferred $1,000 in taxes you would have had to pay had you pocketed the $4,000 instead. In other words, Uncle Sam is paying $1,000 of the $4,000 you have invested in your PCM Co. Your employer also invests $1,200 (50% of your pay up to 6%) in your PCM Co., for a total of $2,200. That's a 73% return on your investment of $3,000 in one year. Guaranteed! After five years, OPM gives you a 99% return; after ten years, a 139% return. And so on. Where else can you get that kind of return on your money? If you're thinking like an entrepreneur, this should get your attention.

Looking out over long periods of time you can see the phenomenal growth on your and your partners' investment. Go to www.paychecksfor life.org and click on the OPM Calculator to model different assumptions and view your results instantaneously.

Your 401(k) provides immediate access to OPM on an interest-free basis. There isn't a bank in the world that will lend you money interest free. If you're serious about creating and managing your own PCM Co., you can't afford to turn down such an offer. OPM is an essential part of the plan. Understand it. Maximize it. And most of all, stick with it.

OPM and the Desirement Mortgage Concept

Let's put what you learned about OPM and Desirement Mortgages together. To do so, we'll use the Desirement Mortgage Calculator again. (Go to www. paychecksforlife.org and click on Desirement Mortgage Calculator.)

In the scenario from the previous chapter we used the following assumptions:

1. Current age: 35
2. Desirement age: 65
3. Needs-based rate of return: 6%
4. Annual income: $40,000
5. Annual raise (inflation): 3%
6. Annual Social Security income: $15,000
7. Desired percentage of income at retirement: 70% ($28,000 annually)
8. Current plan balance: $45,000

Based on these assumptions, our thirty-five-year-old had a desirement number of $696,935.

Going to Step 2 of the calculator, Funding Your Number, shows us his monthly mortgage payment is $690.

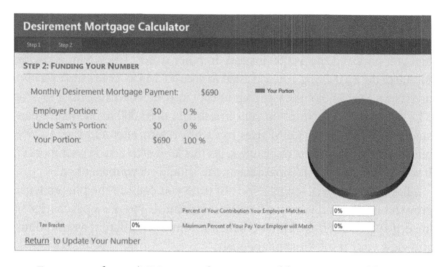

For some of you, $690 a month may seem like an impossible amount of money to save. Let's find out how you can reduce that monthly payment with OPM.

Uncle Sam's Money = OPM

In Principle #3, we learned that if you make your contribution to your PCM Co. on a pre-tax basis, Uncle Sam will fund a percentage of your contribution equal to your tax bracket. In this case, we're assuming the thirty-five-year-old is in a 25% federal tax bracket , which means Uncle Sam is paying $172 per month of his Desirement Mortgage payment, or 25% of the monthly payment.

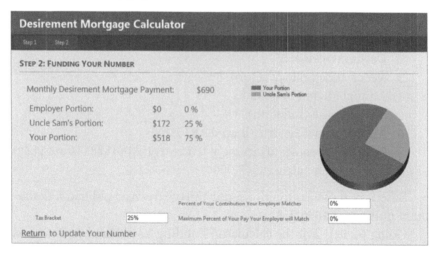

Your Employer's Money (OPM)

Let's find out what your employer is willing to contribute towards your Desirement Mortgage payment. You can find out what your employer match is by reading your 401(K) summary plan description or by speaking to your human resource department. For this example, we'll assume your employer will match 50 cents on every dollar your save in your 401(k) up to the first 6%. This means the employer is contributing $100 per month of your Desirement Mortgage payment, or 14% of the entire monthly payment.

In the Desirement Mortgage Calculator, by entering 50% for the Percent Your Employer Matches and 6% for the Maximum Percent Your Employer Matches, you see the following results.

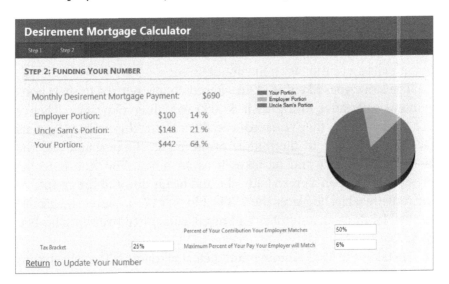

The Magic of OPM

In this example, OPM has reduced the Desirement Mortgage of our thirty-five-year-old by 35%, from $690 per month to $442 per month. That's lower than the average home mortgage payment! On a weekly basis, it's $102 per week or $14.50 per day.

You can use the calculator for your actual situation by inserting the right variables into The Desirement Mortgage Calculator at www. paychecksforlife.org.

The Green Bathrobe Effect

It's important that you're aware of a common mental accounting trap before launching your PCM Co. Many 401(k) participants tend to think that because they have access to OPM, they should take unnecessary risks. After all, if it's not your money, why not roll the dice and reach your desirement goals even earlier?

Gary Belsky and Thomas Gilovich explain why that thinking is a critical mistake in their book *Why Smart People Make Big Money Mistakes and How to Correct Them*. They illustrate their point with an urban legend often told near Las Vegas casinos: "The Legend of the Man in the Green Bathrobe." Whether gamblers believe the story or not, it makes a cautionary point about OPM.

The story goes like this. A newlywed couple returns to their honeymoon suite after losing their $1,000 gambling allowance. They're not totally broke; they've saved a $5.00 roulette chip with #17 on its face as a souvenir. In the middle of the night, the husband sees the clock flashing 3:17 and he takes it as an omen. Too frantic to get dressed, he puts on a green bathrobe and heads down to the casino. At the roulette table, he places the $5.00 chip on #17, of course. Magically, the ball lands on that number and he collects thirty-five times his bet, or $175.

He takes the $175 winnings and bets it all on #17. The wheel spins and the ball miraculously lands there again. His winnings increase to $6,125. He does this again and again until he's worth $262 million.

He takes the $262 million and bets it all on his shockingly successful number #17. This time, though, Lady Luck deserts him. The ball lands on #18 and the man loses everything. With dampened spirits, he walks back to his hotel room.

"Where were you?" asks the bride.

"Playing roulette," he replies.

"How did you do?" she asks.

"Not bad," he responds. "I only lost $5.00."

While the story makes a strong point in a humorous and exaggerated way, think seriously about where the error lies. While the groom's accounting methods may be acceptable for government use, I hope you agree that his loss was far more than $5.00. Even though he leveraged his money into $262 million doesn't mean that it had no value. Believing those millions have no value (or less value) is called a mental accounting trap.

While most investors agree that $5.00 is not his total loss, they make identical accounting errors with investing. For some reason, investors often feel that some dollars are worth more because of where they come from. They treat their own dollars with respect, but OPM dollars as free money. Don't fall for that. Just because other people contribute money to your PCM Co. doesn't mean their money isn't real.

Other people's money is real. If you treat it as anything less, I'll send you a green bathrobe.

PAYCHECKS FOR LIFE ACTION STEPS

☐ You must make OPM part of your plan if you wish to create a steady stream of paychecks for life.

☐ There are two partners in your PCM Co. ready and willing to invest their capital in your business: Uncle Sam and your employer.

☐ Uncles Sam's Money (USM) is offered to you interest free. You can either take it now and invest it in your PCM Co. or let Uncle Sam keep it, never to be seen again.

☐ Your Employer's Money (YEM) may be a matching contribution. YEM not only is interest free, but does not have to be repaid after six years. Think of YEM like a raise. If your employer offers a 6% match, you should contribute the full 6%. If the company offers 10%, contribute the 10%. Don't let your employer keep any of its matching contribution. It's free, so take it.

☐ The combined power of USM and YEM could mean a guaranteed 50% to 150% return on the money you contribute to your PCM Co. every year.

☐ Think of your desirement mortgage the same way you do your home mortgage. Use the lowest interest rate possible and sleep at night. Treat it with respect. Never gamble with it.

☐ Even when times are bad and markets are down, keep making your desirement mortgage payment just like you do your home mortgage payment.

☐ Just because other people contribute money to your PCM Co. doesn't mean their money isn't real.

☐ Use the Desirement Mortgage Calculator located at the website www.paychecksforlife.org to determine how much of your desirement mortgage Uncle Sam and your employer will pay each month.

Principle #4

Harness the Power of Compound Interest

Mother Nature can certainly unleash forces that command respect. Tornadoes, hurricanes, volcanoes, and earthquakes can all have devastating effects. None, however, match the power of compound interest. Rumor has it that Albert Einstein once called compound interest "the most powerful force in the universe." The power of compound interest isn't just appreciated by scientists. In 1990, during one of his memorable monologues on *The Tonight Show*, Johnny Carson joked that "scientists have developed a powerful new weapon that destroys people but leaves buildings standing. It's called the 17% interest rate." Both are compelling statements about the power of compounding; it must command respect. Its force is indisputable.

Of course, whether it's a good or bad force depends on which side of the transaction you're on. If you're paying high compound interest rates, such as on credit card debt, it can take years to pay off a relatively small balance if you make only the minimum payment. If, however, you can harness the power of compounding for your investments, it can work magic over time. The best news is that compound interest is available to you in your PCM Co. It's a critical asset of the company and is available to you in unlimited quantities. But you must understand it in order to use it, and you must begin using it as quickly as possible.

Investments earn money and then they earn money on that money. And then that money earns money. It's like a snowball rolling downhill. The longer it rolls, the bigger it gets and the faster it grows.

To demonstrate the power of compounding, here's a little thought experiment you can try. Start with a stack of pennies and a checkerboard. Place one penny on the first square and double it as you move to each successive square. You'll have two pennies on the second square, four on the third, eight on the forth, and so on. How much money will you have on the final square? Ready for the answer?

Most people guess in the hundreds of thousands of dollars. A daring few will guess a couple of million dollars. While both of those answers would certainly make the point about the power of compounding, they're not even remotely close. The point is much stronger.

The amount of money on that board is so big that it's difficult to break down into a meaningful amount. Here's one way to do it: at the end of 2009, the national debt was about $12 trillion, an amount too big to comprehend. However, the amount of money on that board is over 8,000 times greater still.

As I mentioned, the number is so large that it's difficult to conceptualize, so here's another way to wrap your brain around it. Microsoft Chairman Bill Gates's highest net worth, in 1998, was around $92 billion. The number of dollars on the final square of the checkerboard would be more than a million times bigger. If you think Bill Gates is wealthy, imagine a million times his net worth.

What do you suppose would happen to your PCM Co. if you could access the power of compounding to generate growth on your capital and OPM? To help answer this question, consider simple interest first.

Simple Interest

Whenever you deposit money to an account, it's called the "principal." Assume you deposit $1,000 cash at a bank that promises to pay 5% simple interest per year. Simple interest means the bank will calculate your interest payments based on that initial deposit only. In one year, your account will earn $50 interest, bringing the balance to $1,050. If you leave your money in that same bank for another year, you'll earn another $50 in interest, making your balance $1,100. Each year the bank simply pays 5% on the original $1,000 balance. It doesn't matter how big the account gets over time. As long as you never deposit more money to the account, you'll earn $50 per year. Simple interest is paid only on the principal balance—the amount you initially invested.

The formula to calculate simple interest is *principal* × *rate* × *time*. *Principal* is the amount of money on which interest will be calculated ($1,000 in the previous example). *Rate* is the interest rate expressed as a decimal (5% would be 0.05). *Time* is the number of years the deposit will be held.

Using the formula, the simple interest on $1,000 invested at a rate of 5% for five years would be $250 ($1,000 × 0.05 × 5), for a total account value of $1,250.

The main thing to understand about simple interest is that it is a fixed amount of interest each year; it never changes regardless of how big the account balance may get. Compound interest doesn't work that way.

Compound Interest

We just saw how interest is added each year when calculated under the simple interest formula. If interest is compounded, you earn interest on the principal *and* on the interest.

Let's go back to the previous example and assume you deposited $1,000 into a bank that pays 5% compound interest per year. After the first year, your account will be worth $1,050 just as it would be with simple interest; however, in the second year, you'll be paid 5% on your entire $1,050 balance. In other words, you'll earn interest on your $1,000 principal and on the $50 interest paid in the first year. This means your account will gain another $52.50 ($1,050 × 0.05) of interest, bringing your balance to $1,102.50.

> **"If interest is compounded, you earn interest on the principal and on the interest."**

With simple interest, the account balance after two years was $1,100. Although the compound interest balance is only $2.50 higher after year two, the difference gets magnified as time goes on, just as with a snowball rolling downhill: the snowball collects snow and then that snow collects snow. That's the power of compounding.

There is, of course, a formula you can use to find the answers to more complicated questions involving compound interest: *account value = principal* $\times$ $(1 + rate)^{time}$.

Using this formula, the total account value of $1,000 invested at 5% compound interest after two years would be $1,276.28 ($1,000 $\times$ [1 + 0.05]^5). Compare this to the simple interest account balance of $1,250.

Here's another important point: it's in the final years when the interest on the interest surpasses the interest on the principal. As seen in the figure below, the portion of the account value due to compounding (dark bars) eventually exceeds that due to simple interest (grey bars)—if you allow enough time.

The Power of Interest on Interest

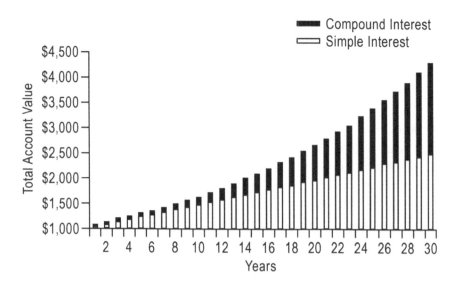

It's this acceleration in the final years that makes compounding such an incredible force. We can see it in action if we analyze the results from the checkerboard puzzle. For example, on the eighth square, your total is only $1.29. You'll have about $328 on the sixteenth square and $83,886 on the twenty-fourth square. The checkerboard has only sixty-four squares, so it's hard to believe the last square will have quadrillions of dollars sitting on it. But it will. It all happens in the last few squares, when the compounding force takes powerful effect.

Similarly, the final years make all the difference in the world for your PCM Co. Time is the greatest asset you have when investing. Like OPM, it's one of your greatest allies in creating paychecks for life. The longer the time, the longer the power of compounding can work. It pays to start your PCM Co. today.

The Rule of Seventy-Two
Another quick formula for determining how quickly your money can grow is known as the rule of seventy-two. To determine how fast your money will double, take the rate of interest and divide it by seventy-two.

For example, in the previous chapter we assumed a needs-based rate of return of 6% per year. The rule of seventy-two says that money invested at this rate will double every twelve years (72/6 = 12).

The Cost of Waiting
I have heard many younger people say "I am too young to start a PCM Co.," or "I'll start when I'm older," or "I still have plenty of time, what's the big deal?" The big deal is this: the earlier you start, the wealthier you finish.

"The earlier you start, the wealthier you finish."

Take the stories of Susan, George, and Morgan on the following page. When they start investing, Susan is twenty-one, George, thirty-one, and Morgan, forty-one. Each earns $40,000 a year and each saves 10% of his or her paycheck per year. Each earns a compounded rate of return of 7% each year, and all of them have set sixty-five as their desirement age.

Start Early and Finish Wealthy

Savings Rate: $4,000
Average Rate of Return: 7.00%

	Susan			George			Morgan	
Age	Total Saved	Balance	Age	Total Saved	Balance	Age	Total Saved	Balance
21	$4,000	$4,000	21			21		
22	$8,000	$8,280	22			22		
23	$12,000	$12,860	23			23		
24	$16,000	$17,760	24			24		
25	$20,000	$23,003	25			25		
26	$24,000	$28,613	26			26		
27	$28,000	$34,616	27			27		
28	$32,000	$41,039	28			28		
29	$36,000	$47,912	29			29		
30	$40,000	$55,266	30			30		
31	$44,000	$63,134	31	$4,000	$4,000	31		
32	$48,000	$71,554	32	$8,000	$8,280	32		
33	$52,000	$80,563	33	$12,000	$12,860	33		
34	$56,000	$90,202	34	$16,000	$17,760	34		
35	$60,000	$100,516	35	$20,000	$23,003	35		
36	$64,000	$111,552	36	$24,000	$28,613	36		
37	$68,000	$123,361	37	$28,000	$34,616	37		
38	$72,000	$135,996	38	$32,000	$41,039	38		
39	$76,000	$149,516	39	$36,000	$47,912	39		
40	$80,000	$163,982	40	$40,000	$55,266	40		
41	$84,000	$179,461	41	$44,000	$63,134	41	$4,000	$4,000
42	$88,000	$196,023	42	$48,000	$71,554	42	$8,000	$8,280
43	$92,000	$213,745	43	$52,000	$80,563	43	$12,000	$12,860
44	$96,000	$232,707	44	$56,000	$90,202	44	$16,000	$17,760
45	$100,000	$252,996	45	$60,000	$100,516	45	$20,000	$23,003
46	$104,000	$274,706	46	$64,000	$111,552	46	$24,000	$28,613
47	$108,000	$297,935	47	$68,000	$123,361	47	$28,000	$34,616
48	$112,000	$322,791	48	$72,000	$135,996	48	$32,000	$41,039
49	$116,000	$349,386	49	$76,000	$149,516	49	$36,000	$47,912
50	$120,000	$377,843	50	$80,000	$163,982	50	$40,000	$55,266
51	$124,000	$408,292	51	$84,000	$179,461	51	$44,000	$63,134
52	$128,000	$440,873	52	$88,000	$196,023	52	$48,000	$71,554
53	$132,000	$475,734	53	$92,000	$213,745	53	$52,000	$80,563
54	$136,000	$513,035	54	$96,000	$232,707	54	$56,000	$90,202
55	$140,000	$552,948	55	$100,000	$252,996	55	$60,000	$100,516
56	$144,000	$595,654	56	$104,000	$274,706	56	$64,000	$111,552
57	$148,000	$641,350	57	$108,000	$297,935	57	$68,000	$123,361
58	$152,000	$690,244	58	$112,000	$322,791	58	$72,000	$135,996
59	$156,000	$742,561	59	$116,000	$349,386	59	$76,000	$149,516
60	$160,000	$798,540	60	$120,000	$377,843	60	$80,000	$163,982
61	$164,000	$858,438	61	$124,000	$408,292	61	$84,000	$179,461
62	$168,000	$922,529	62	$128,000	$440,873	62	$88,000	$196,023
63	$172,000	$991,106	63	$132,000	$475,734	63	$92,000	$213,745
64	$176,000	$1,064,483	64	$136,000	$513,035	64	$96,000	$232,707
65	$180,000	$1,142,997	65	$140,000	$552,948	65	$100,000	$252,996

What an amazing result for Susan. She starts just ten years before George, invests $40,000 more, but ends up with $590,049 more money than him and $890,001 more than Morgan. Put another way, Susan earned 375% more on the $40,000 she invested in the first 10 years, before George and Morgan started investing.

The Power of OPM and Compound Interest Combined

Remember what we learned in Principle #1 about marginal thinking and about how acting like an entrepreneur helps you operate and manage your 401(k)—that is, your PCM Co.? Remember what we learned in Principle #3 about OPM? As you can see, compound interest combined with the power of OPM is really marginal thinking on steroids. Small increments of time have an enormous impact on your results.

> "As you can see, compound interest combined with the power of OPM is really marginal thinking on steroids. Small increments of time have an enormous impact on your results."

Triple Duty Dollars

Your PCM Co. offers you what I call triple duty dollars. All three investors, in the previous table, had three powerful benefits. First, they were able to invest 100% of their $4,000 contribution because they contributed the money "pre-tax." Second, they did not have to pay taxes on their 7% earnings each year. Third, they captured the power of compound interest on their entire investment each year. That's a dollar working three-times, or a triple duty dollar and marginal thinking on steroids.

In contrast, take a look at the following table. Here all three investors lose the benefit of Uncle Sam's $1,000 tax savings, because they choose to invest outside of their PCM Co. In addition they have to pay taxes on their earnings each year. And finally the power of compound interest is reduced exponentially.

The Loss of Triple Duty Dollars

Savings Rate: $3,000
Average Rate of Return: 5.25%

	Susan			George			Morgan	
Age	Total Saved	Balance	Age	Total Saved	Balance	Age	Total Saved	Balance
21	$3,000	$3,000	21			21		
22	$6,000	$6,158	22			22		
23	$9,000	$9,481	23			23		
24	$12,000	$12,979	24			24		
25	$15,000	$16,660	25			25		
26	$18,000	$20,535	26			26		
27	$21,000	$24,613	27			27		
28	$24,000	$28,905	28			28		
29	$27,000	$33,422	29			29		
30	$30,000	$38,177	30			30		
31	$33,000	$43,181	31	$3,000	$3,000	31		
32	$36,000	$48,448	32	$6,000	$6,158	32		
33	$39,000	$53,992	33	$9,000	$9,481	33		
34	$42,000	$59,826	34	$12,000	$12,979	34		
35	$45,000	$65,967	35	$15,000	$16,660	35		
36	$48,000	$72,430	36	$18,000	$20,158	36		
37	$51,000	$79,233	37	$21,000	$24,613	37		
38	$54,000	$86,393	38	$24,000	$28,905	38		
39	$57,000	$93,928	39	$27,000	$33,422	39		
40	$60,000	$101,860	40	$30,000	$38,177	40		
41	$63,000	$110,207	41	$33,000	$43,181	41	$3,000	$3,000
42	$66,000	$118,993	42	$36,000	$48,448	42	$6,000	$6,158
43	$69,000	$128,240	43	$39,000	$53,992	43	$9,000	$9,481
44	$72,000	$137,973	44	$42,000	$59,826	44	$12,000	$12,979
45	$75,000	$148,217	45	$45,000	$65,967	45	$15,000	$16,660
46	$78,000	$158,998	46	$48,000	$72,430	46	$18,000	$20,535
47	$81,000	$170,345	47	$51,000	$79,233	47	$21,000	$24,613
48	$84,000	$182,288	48	$54,000	$86,393	48	$24,000	$28,905
49	$87,000	$194,859	49	$57,000	$93,928	49	$27,000	$33,422
50	$90,000	$208,089	50	$60,000	$101,860	50	$30,000	$38,177
51	$93,000	$222,013	51	$63,000	$110,207	51	$33,000	$43,181
52	$96,000	$236,669	52	$66,000	$118,993	52	$36,000	$48,448
53	$99,000	$252,094	53	$69,000	$128,240	53	$39,000	$53,992
54	$102,000	$268,329	54	$72,000	$137,973	54	$42,000	$59,826
55	$105,000	$285,416	55	$75,000	$148,217	55	$45,000	$65,967
56	$108,000	$303,401	56	$78,000	$158,998	56	$48,000	$72,430
57	$111,000	$322,329	57	$81,000	$170,345	57	$51,000	$79,233
58	$114,000	$342,251	58	$84,000	$182,288	58	$54,000	$86,393
59	$117,000	$363,220	59	$87,000	$194,859	59	$57,000	$93,928
60	$120,000	$385,289	60	$90,000	$208,089	60	$60,000	$101,860
61	$123,000	$408,516	61	$93,000	$222,013	61	$63,000	$110,207
62	$126,000	$432,964	62	$96,000	$236,669	62	$66,000	$118,993
63	$129,000	$458,694	63	$99,000	$252,094	63	$69,000	$128,240
64	$132,000	$485,776	64	$102,000	$268,329	64	$72,000	$137,973
65	$135,000	$514,279	65	$105,000	$285,416	65	$75,000	$148,217

The results for Susan, George and Morgan, between the table Start Early and Finish Wealthy (where they all invested inside their Paycheck Manufacturing Co), versus the table The Loss of Triple Duty Dollars (where they chose to invest with after tax dollars "outside" their Paycheck Manufacturing Co) are astounding.

Inside her Paycheck Manufacturing Co, Susan would have accumulated $1,142,997 versus $514,279 outside her PCM Co. A $628,718 difference! For George the difference is $267,532 and for Morgan $104,779, still nothing to sneeze about!

10–1–NOW

I have a very simple mantra that I chant at all of my 401(k) educational meetings. It's "10–1–NOW."

The "10" stands for "save 10% of your pay." As a rule of thumb, if you invest 10% of your pay in your PCM Co., you'll accumulate enough capital to generate paychecks for life. (This is a simple rule of thumb that depends on how old you are and whether you hold other assets outside your PCM Co. that can contribute to generating your paychecks for life).

The "1" stands for "if you can't save 10% now, increase your contribution to your PCM Co. by 1% of your earnings each year until you get to 10%." You have already seen in the previous examples how important starting early can be to your results. But people often tell me they can't afford to save 10% of their pay right now because they have other bills to pay. To this I say, you must contribute up to your company's match. Don't give up YEM. If your company's matching contribution is 100% up to the first 4%, you *must* invest 4% of your paycheck to get all of the YEM available to you. If the match is 50% on the first 6%, you *must* invest 6% of your paycheck. Pretty simple.

But don't stop there. Every year thereafter, increase your contribution by just 1%. One measly percent. Remember that with compound interest on your side, increasing your investment in your PCM Co. by just 1% a year makes an enormous difference. Don't just believe me; take a look at the following table.

The 10-1-Now table shows that Susan, George, and Morgan all start to contribute at the same time. Susan contributes 10% per year, George contributes 5% the first year and increases his contribution by 1% until he gets to 10% in year six, and Morgan just contributes 5% every year.

10–1–NOW

Base Salary: $40,000
Average Rate of Return: 6.00%
Average Salary Increase: 0.00%

Year	10% per year Susan			5% Now + 1%/yr until 10% George			5% forever Morgan		
	Annual Savings	Earnings	Balance	Annual Savings	Earnings	Balance	Annual Savings	Earnings	Balance
1	$4,000	$0	$4,000	$2,000	$0	$2,000	$2,000	$0	$2,000
5	$4,000	$1,050	$22,548	$3,600	$675	$15,521	$2,000	$525	$11,274
10	$4,000	$2,758	$52,723	$4,000	$2,226	$43,320	$2,000	$1,379	$26,362
15	$4,000	$5,044	$93,104	$4,000	$4,331	$80,520	$2,000	$2,522	$46,552
20	$4,000	$8,102	$147,142	$4,000	$7,149	$130,302	$2,000	$4,051	$73,571
25	$4,000	$12,196	$219,458	$4,000	$10,920	$196,922	$2,000	$6,098	$109,729
30	$4,000	$17,674	$316,233	$4,000	$15,966	$286,074	$2,000	$8,837	$158,116
35	$4,000	$25,004	$445,739	$4,000	$22,720	$405,380	$2,000	$12,502	$222,870
40	$4,000	$34,814	$619,048	$4,000	$31,757	$565,039	$2,000	$17,407	$309,524
45	$4,000	$47,942	$850,974	$4,000	$43,851	$778,697	$2,000	$23,971	$425,487
50	$4,000	$65,510	$1,161,344	$4,000	$60,035	$1,064,621	$2,000	$32,755	$580,672

In forty years, Susan ends up with $619,048. George, who said, "I can't contribute 10% to start," but who increases his contributions incrementally, ends with $565,039, only $54,009 less than Susan. Not bad, especially compared with Morgan, who never increases her percentage and ends up with $309,524, or 50% less than Susan. This is marginal thinking at work once again. George makes a marginal improvement in his business each year by increasing his contribution to his PCM Co. He invests a total of $64,000 more than Morgan, but has $255,515 more for his desirement years.

Principle #5 is about how you can automatically set in place my 10–1–NOW mantra. For now, review the tables in this chapter and let the power of compound interest get under your skin and motivate you to take action NOW to increase your investment in your PCM Co.

I've demonstrated the mechanics of simple and compound interest with a hypothetical bank account. What does that have to do with the 401(k) investments you're likely to make in mutual funds? Even though mutual funds do not pay annual interest as in these examples, they do have returns in the sense that their values tend to rise over time. If you invest $1,000 in a mutual fund that rises by 5% in a year, it's worth $1,050. If it rises 5% again the next year, it's worth $1,102.50 ($1,050 × 1.05), just as in the compound interest example. So while mutual funds do not actually pay interest in the same way a bank does, their compounded gains affect your account balance.

Just as the tortoise proved to the hare in one of *Aesop's Fables*, slow and steady wins the race. A little entrepreneurship combined with a long-term, steady application of marginal thinking will generate magnificent paychecks for life. Compounding makes it all possible. The sooner you begin, the sooner you'll earn money—and the sooner that money will earn money on money. Remember the penny's compounding power.

PAYCHECKS FOR LIFE ACTION STEPS

☐ The sooner you start contributing your money and OPM into your PCM Co., the sooner you'll witness the power of compound interest.

☐ Slow and steady wins the race. Compounding takes a while to get started, but once it does, the process accelerates and your savings grow more substantially each year.

☐ The final years of compounding make all the difference in the value of your PCM Co. Time is the greatest asset you have in investing.

☐ Small contributions compounded for twenty years can make you the millionaire next door.

☐ Put the power of marginal thinking and my 10–1–NOW mantra to work today. If you can't invest 10% of your pay to begin with, start with what you can and increase it by 1% of your earnings every year.

Sara and Barry Roberts

A Cautionary Tale

It was the beginning of 2000. The Y2K scare had passed without incident, and the Dow Jones Industrial Average had closed above 11,500 for the first time in history. It was the peak of the dot-com obsession, and the market was setting new highs, acting like a runaway train under the guise of the "new economy" supposedly created by all the rapid changes in technology.

I was beginning the year by making my usual visits to companies whose 401(k) plans were managed by my firm. We had just taken on the investment oversight and management of a new client's 401(k) plan, and I was conducting one of our Paychecks for Life seminars for its sixty employees. Seated in the front row was a woman who was listening intently and taking lots of notes.

After the workshop, she approached me. Her name was Sara Roberts, an office administrator who had worked with the company for nearly eighteen years. She wanted to set up an appointment to talk about her financial situation. Considering her many years with the company, I thought she must be worth a small fortune, but when I questioned her I found out she wasn't participating in the 401(k).

Two weeks later, Sara and her husband, Barry, came to my office. Barry was a fifty-two-year-old pilot who had worked for nearly twenty years with a major airline. He was tall and handsome and carried that confident aura that's characteristic of pilots. Upon meeting him, you'd know instantly he was the kind of guy you wanted in the cockpit when, at 35,000 feet, your plane hit major turbulence.

"Look," Barry said almost immediately. "No disrespect, but I'm not sure why we're here. Sara said she attended your session on something called paychecks for life, but I have to tell you, even though I'm here, I'm highly confident in our retirement plans and the safe strategies we've had in place for the last twenty years."

"That's fine," I said. "Many people I meet with for the first time already have a plan in place and are confident with their investment strategies. To be honest, what really interested me about the two of you was the fact that Sara has been employed at her company for nearly eighteen years yet has never invested a single penny in the company-sponsored 401(k) plan. Now that I hear you already have a plan in place, I would love to learn more about it."

As we continued to talk, I learned the Roberts had been married for almost twenty-five years. They had two children: Barry Jr., age twenty, a sophomore in college; and Jordan, sixteen, a junior in high school. Both had attended private schools since kindergarten. "Education has always been one of the most important goals for us," said Sara.

"Yes," Barry added. "My dad was a laborer, working long hours in manufacturing all his life. He worked for the same company for almost forty years and retired with a full pension. Unfortunately, a bad diet and the grueling factory work cut short his retirement. He passed away when he was sixty-nine. His dream was that my brother and I would get a great education and achieve a better life. His wish was for us to work with our heads, not our backs. I have always been careful with our finances to make sure his wishes come true for us and our children."

"We purchased our first home almost twenty years ago," Sara added. "It was a modest house at first, and our mortgage payment was small. As the kids came along, we put a couple of additions on the house. Our mortgage payment increased, but as a percentage of our growing salary it remained relatively small. With interest rates low in the late 1980s and early 1990s, we managed to refinance several times and keep our payment at less than 25% of our net pay."

"Very impressive," I said. "That's far below the average bank limits for mortgage debt."

"Our goal is to have the house paid off in ten years when Barry is sixty-two," Sara said.

"Just in time for me to retire comfortably and pursue my love for fixing up old cars and hot rods. It's my dad's mechanical ghost inside me," Barry chuckled.

"While he's playing with his toys, I'm hoping to enjoy all my outdoor interests and, with any luck, with grandkids as well," Sara added.

"Wow, that's great, and inspiring," I said. "It sounds like you know exactly what you want to do."

Next, Sara pulled out the financial documents I had asked them to bring. Their tax return for the prior year (1999) showed Barry's income at $140,000 and Sara's at $34,500, for a combined income of $174,500. While not exorbitant, it was certainly well above the median household income, which, according to the 1998 U.S. Census, stood at $38,885 per year for two-income households.

A quick look at their financial statements revealed they were blessed there as well. There was a relatively small mortgage of $83,000 on their home. A second home in Montana, however, had a larger mortgage balance: $220,000. "A home in Montana!" I exclaimed. "That sounds beautiful."

"We love the outdoors," started Sara. "Fly-fishing, kayaking, and hunting in the warm months. Skiing and snowshoeing in the winter months. It's our winter getaway home now, but when we retire it will be our permanent home."

I introduced the idea of a desirement wish list and asked them what else they'd like to put on it. "Starting a small flight school should be added to my list," Barry said with a burst of adrenaline in his voice.

"Going to culinary school for me," added Sara.

"She's already a great cook," Barry smiled, patting his stomach.

"Exactly," I said. "Now you're getting the idea. You need to stretch your imaginations and realize that your desirement wish list never ends. It's something you'll always be adding to and updating as you continue to dream about, talk about, and experiment with a bigger future for yourselves and your family.

"Please close your eyes for a moment," I continued. Both Sara and Barry closed their eyes. "Now think back to the time just before you bought your first house. You dreamed about it, probably talked about it, and then started looking at houses until finally, one day, you found that first house of your dreams."

"It was on 28 Ardsley Terrace," said Sara. "I'll never forget seeing it for the first time with our realtor. Barry was on a flight, and I couldn't wait to call him when he landed."

"Yes. She met me at the airport when I landed and dragged me to see it before I could even change out of my uniform."

"We made an offer the next day!" exclaimed Sara.

"When you went to the bank closing to purchase the house, how much did it cost?" I asked.

"Two hundred and seventy-five thousand dollars," said Barry.

"And when you went to the closing," I continued, "did you bring $275,000 of your own money in cash?"

"Are you kidding? We barely scraped up the required 20% down payment and took out a mortgage for the remaining $220,000."

"And what was the term and rate of your mortgage?" I asked.

"Thirty years at an original rate of 10.5%," responded Barry.

"No, honey," Sara corrected him. "It was 9.5%. The rates had just come down from their all-time highs. We waited two extra weeks and the rates dropped from 10.0% to 9.5%."

"I believe you're right," Barry said. "Of course, we've re-mortgaged the house several times thereafter when we built the two additions. But I think we got the rate down to an unbelievable 5%."

"And why did you take out a thirty-year mortgage and keep refinancing at lower rates?" I asked.

"So we could have the lowest fixed monthly payment and reduce our monthly costs," he answered slowly, looking at me as if he thought I was asking him a trick question.

"Well now," I said. "Everything you've just described is similar to what I call a desirement mortgage."

"What's that?" Barry and Sara asked together.

"It's just like your house mortgage," I answered. "You add the cost of all the things you desire to do when you stop working, and you put a lump-sum price tag on it. Then we simply calculate how much money you'd need to save each month, like your mortgage payment, based on a fixed rate of interest to create a sum of money that will then generate the paychecks for life you'll need to pay for all those desirement years."

"I'd never thought of it that way," said Barry, pondering my idea. "It sounds great, but I'm sure the plan we have in place right now will create those paychecks and that desirement mortgage for us."

It was evident that the Roberts believed they had a crystal-clear vision for their retirement years—certainly one with a brighter ending than Barry's father—so I said enthusiastically, "Can you tell me a little more about your current investing plans? Why are you so confident in your ability to retire successfully on time?"

I looked closely at Barry and Sara's plan, and here is what I found. They were counting on the fact that when Barry reached sixty-two he'd receive two incomes, one from his company's pension plan and the other from Social Security. Barry would have thirty years with his current company by then, and his employer's pension plan would pay him 70% of the average of his income for the last three years.

Assuming his current income of $140,000 grew by 3% inflation, his income at age sixty-one would be approximately $183,000. His average three-year income from age fifty-nine to sixty-one would be approximately $177,000, so his pension income would be 70% of that, or $124,000 per year.

When Barry reached age sixty-two, he also expected to receive $2,150 per month, or $25,800 annually, from Social Security. Sara expected $1,250 month or $15,000 annually, for a yearly total of $40,800.

Unlike Barry's company, Sara's didn't have a pension plan, only the 401(k) plan to which she had never contributed. Barry's airline had a 401(k) plan as well, but he had also chosen not to contribute to it. He had always felt his company's pension plan along with both of their Social Security benefits would generate enough money for them at retirement.

Indeed it was difficult, at first glance, to argue with the Roberts's approach. The combined projected income from Barry's yearly pension of $124,000 and their annual Social Security benefits of $40,800 would be $164,800, a substantial sum by any stretch of the imagination. In addition, Barry and Sara had also managed over the years to accumulate $100,000 in the bank. Barry had $85,000 of it invested in a global technology mutual fund that Barry's pilot friends had recommended; they were convinced it would grow 20% per year until he retired.

Despite Barry's confidence in his master plan, I began explaining how their 401(k) plans were really their own Paycheck Manufacturing Companies. The power of marginal thinking and compound interest were already working in Barry's pension plan, "so why not put these same concepts to work in a business you both will own," I explained.

I pointed out that they'd been passing up the powerful benefits of OPM (their companies' matching programs, which were dollar-for-dollar of the first 6%, and Uncle Sam's tax savings) for the past thirty years. Had they been saving just 10% of their pay and earning compound interest on their employers' generous match, they would have had more money than the Stevens's, since their incomes were almost twice as high. The decision to rely on Social Security and Barry's pension plan, which they had no control over, had already cost them over a million dollars in lost contributions and compound interest in their PCM Co.

"Start investing now," I urged them. "Max out your contributions and your companies' matching programs." In 2000, that meant they could each contribute $10,500 (this amount would gradually increase to $16,500 in 2009, plus the $5,500 catch-up provision). This represented a significant way to grow their PCM Cos. as quickly as possible and accumulate additional wealth that could be used to fund their lifetime paychecks. Assuming they lived to life expectancy (age eighty-five) and earned simple 5% compound interest on their money, they would accumulate another million dollars to fund their desirement years.

I felt strongly that I had laid out the benefits of contributing to their respective 401(k) plans and becoming entrepreneurs of their own PCM Cos. rather than employees entitled only to outdated pension and government benefits. If they followed my recommendations and took advantage of the power of triple duty OPM dollars, over their lifetimes they would accumulate over $2 million in their PCM Cos.

"Your companies' matching contributions alone provide returns on your money that you can't find anywhere else," I preached. "The financial rewards are too great to pass up. You never know what risks lie ahead and there's no better time than the present to take command of your financial future."

"Maybe so," said Barry, "but I've already got OPM working for me in my company's guaranteed pension plan and the government's guaranteed Social Security benefits. Why should we bother to invest our own money?" He stood up to shake my hand and thanked me for my time.

Sara smiled and thanked me warmly as well. "I've learned a lot," she said. "Let's stay in touch. You never know what the future holds."

Little did I or the Roberts's know how much truth Sara's last words would carry. No one could have imagined the financial storm clouds that were gathering, which in less than twenty-four months would shatter the couple's confidence and financial security. While Barry may be able to handle turbulence well on the flight deck, the looming financial turbulence would prove to be out of his control.

After they left my office that day, it occurred to me that even though Barry felt he was in control of his financial future, he was not in command of the outcome, and there's a tremendous difference. Just as the pilot controls a plane's flight plan, it's the control tower that dictates the course the plane takes, and ultimately it's Mother Nature and the forces of unforeseen weather that dictate what happens to an airplane's true course and safety. Little did Barry realize how looming financial forces would soon take command of his financial plans and put them into a tailspin.

Three years after our first meeting, Barry and Sara were once again sitting in my office—only this time everything had changed. Physically, Barry was not the same man. He looked like he had aged twenty years. Even his handshake when he greeted me was noticeably weaker. The tech bubble that had created record expansion between 1992 and 2000 had burst. Daily news stories were breaking about rampant corporate corruption, and the Dow was trading below 8,000, down nearly 32% from its 11,700 high in January 2000.

The 9/11 attacks in 2001 were tragic enough, but the ripple effects had been devastating for the airline industry—and for Barry. First, Barry's hours were cut back with the reduction in air traffic. Then, faced with piling debts, the airline he worked for was forced to file Chapter 11 bankruptcy. Management told Barry that even if the company came out of the mess, employee pensions were gone. Even with government pension insurance, he'd be lucky if he saw a fraction of his expected pension.

"I had it all figured out," Barry reminisced, sitting in my office that fall day in 2003. "My pension was going to give me $124,000 a year at age sixty-two, but now I'll be lucky if I see any of that. And who knows if there will be enough money in the Social Security system in ten years to pay our benefits now that the government is forced to spend billions of dollars fighting terrorism all over the world. It's a mess. Maybe we should have listened to your ideas when we first met rather than relying on my company and the government to take care of us in our desirement years."

Barry looked up at me. "So what do we do now, Coach? How do we catch up?"

> *"People who try to catch up (in their 401(k)s) are indirectly asking to accept more risk."*

Catch up? Those are the two words I dread hearing most as The 401(k) Coach. People who try to catch up are going to take more risk in their investments than they should. Since their previous choice not to start investing in their PCM Cos. has left them behind the eight ball, they believe the only way to catch up is to seek higher returns. They'll do anything to get their portfolio balances up to where they would have been. That's not planning for a financially secure future—that's gambling on your future.

Barry and Sara greatly underestimated the money they were giving up by choosing not to build their own PCM Cos. inside their employers. For nearly eighteen years, they could have invested their money and capitalized on OPM from Uncle Sam and their employers. Had they done that, they'd have accumulated in excess of $1,000,000 in their accounts. It was a costly decision on their part to rely too heavily on government entitlement programs and long-term corporate promises.

If there's one message to take away from the Roberts's experience, it's to take both command and control of your finances *now*. Don't rely solely on government programs, like Social Security, that may not be here in the future, nor on a company-sponsored pension plan. Both are conditional promises that, as we have already discussed, continue to be reduced, taxed away, or taken away altogether. You must take command *and* control of your financial future by building a Paycheck Manufacturing Company that you manage and own and can sell one day to generate paychecks for life. Your 401(k) represents one of the best mechanisms to do this. If you haven't started to build your PCM Co., let the Roberts's story be your wake-up call, and begin 10–1–NOW.

Turn to the next chapter to learn how Principle #5 can automate the building of your PCM Co.

Principle #5

Use Technology to Save Automatically

Emotions can be heated. Emotions can run cool. Emotions can energize you to overcome seemingly impossible challenges, and they can cause you to collapse under intense pressure. Emotions can be an asset or they can be a liability. But one thing is for sure: emotions are always there.

Whether emotions are good or bad depends a lot on the person and the situation, with one exception: money. It's a widely held principle among professional investment advisors that emotions provide no benefit when it comes to investing. Investments are driven by fear and greed, and these two emotions don't mix. Emotions make you falsely attached to your high-performing funds and tell you to stay away from low-performing funds. They cause false hope. They ignore danger. To put it bluntly, they cause you to do financially stupid stuff.

Let's look at just a few emotions that, left unchecked, will greatly threaten the success of your PCM Co.

Emotions at Play in Investing

Overconfidence

Studies have shown that when people are asked to rate their level of expertise in a variety of areas, including finance, the majority rate themselves above average—a mathematical impossibility. Overconfidence makes investors believe that the success they achieve is due solely to their decisions and that they have the ability to do it again. That's a mistaken belief, and one that's difficult for investors to let go of.

Availability Bias

Investors can also project their outlooks too far into the future and let that bias their decision making. A classic example of this occurred in December 1996 when Federal Reserve Chairman Alan Greenspan made a speech to the American Enterprise Institute for Public Policy, where he coined the phrase "irrational exuberance" as a warning that stock market prices were inflated according to fundamental valuations. Few investors listened. They were convinced the market would march higher. After a brief fall, the market continued to climb higher and higher, thus prompting Greenspan to consider that perhaps prices weren't inflated at all. In September 1998 at the Haas Annual Business Faculty Research Dialogue at the University of California, Greenspan said:

> *Some of those who advocate a "new economy" attribute it generally to technological innovations and breakthroughs in globalization that raise productivity and proffer new capacity on demand and that have, accordingly, removed pricing power from the world's producers on a more lasting basis.*

But the more prophetic words from Greenspan came moments later: "There is one important caveat to the notion that we live in a new economy, and that's human psychology."

People were convinced the market would do nothing but continue to climb. And it did—until human psychology took over. From 2000 to 2003, the market shed about 35% of its value, leaving investor accounts in shambles. But from 2003 until the end of 2007, the market gained 86%. Think of the consequences if you were under-diversified when the market was losing 35% because you firmly believed it would continue to grow in the new economy. To make matters worse, what if you sold near the bottom and were afraid to re-enter the market during the subsequent rally? These are very real (and highly likely) situations that occur when investing on emotion.

Risk Aversion

Daniel Kahneman and Amos Tversky, in their book *Choices, Values, and Frames*, showed that people strongly prefer avoiding losses to acquiring gains. In other words, people suffer from risk aversion. The pain felt from a $500 loss is far greater than the satisfaction from a gain of equal size. Therefore, people concentrate their efforts on avoiding losses.

In Kahneman and Tversky's research, a sample of their undergraduates refused to stake $10 on the toss of a coin if they stood to win less than $30. The attractiveness of the gain was not sufficient to compensate for the aversion to the possible loss.

This behavior shouldn't be too surprising, but things got really interesting when the researchers decided to challenge people on their beliefs by adding a related question—with a twist. They asked if people would prefer an 85% chance of losing $1,000 (and, therefore, a 15% chance of losing nothing) or a guaranteed loss of $800. A large majority preferred the gamble over the sure loss. This is risk seeking because the expectation of the gamble is inferior to the expectation of loss.

This shows a critically important point about human psychology and investing: Investors' aversion to losses is so great that it overcomes their aversion to risk. In other words, people despise taking losses so much that they'll overstep their risk boundaries in hopes of avoiding the loss. That's perhaps the most dangerous of all combined approaches you could take to the financial markets. Unfortunately, it's how we're programmed to behave.

Short of wandering aimlessly through the mountains of Tibet searching for a Buddhist monk, can you completely detach from your emotions? Of course not. So what can you do?

Think Like an Entrepreneur: Use Technology to Override Your Emotions

Henry Ford used technology to automate the assembly line for cars, and he changed the world in the process. Michael Dell accomplished a similar feat in building computers with just-in-time production.

Likewise, financial professionals have developed computer programs to handle the rote procedures of financial planning and investing.

Computer trading or program trading, as it's sometimes called, is just what it sounds like—computer programs are doing the buying and selling. Large Wall Street firms may, for example, program a computer to sell one million shares of a particular stock if the Dow reaches 10,000, or buy 20,000 shares of IBM if the price falls below its fifty-day moving average.

Many mutual funds take program trading to a whole new level and allow computers to manage their portfolios by buying or selling shares of particular stocks or indexes as long as certain conditions are met. Profits are taken and losses are limited to specified levels. Rebalancing is automatic. In fact, every single financial decision is automated.

Some financial firms create proprietary computerized systems that individual investors and institutions can access for a fee. These are often called black box systems because they're analogous to an unknown box of rules that makes decisions for you. While these systems often outperform the market, they're expensive and charge access fees of 20% or more of your profits.

Computers are an excellent tool for your PCM Co. because they do things automatically (once instructed) and don't have emotions. You're in the business of financial decisions, and there's no room for the kind of emotions we've already discussed. Let's look at the ways you can automate your PCM Co. and your investment decisions to avoid making costly errors, and override your emotions.

Auto to the 4th Power

What follows are four powerful steps you can take to automate your investing success and take the emotion out of the investing equation. I call these Auto to the 4th Power.

1. Auto Enrollment

In 1998, to encourage people to save for retirement, the Clinton administration created automatic enrollment, which gave companies the right to enroll new employees automatically into their 401(k)s. Although a few major corporations elected to use automatic enrollment, most were reluctant. Many states' laws suggested that corporations could be sued for unauthorized wage withholding or other charges. As a result, despite its good intentions, automatic enrollment didn't catch on at that time. However, new regulations changed that.

Under the *Pension Protection Act* of 2006, corporations are now protected from such suits. No employer can be sued for automatically enrolling an employee into the 401(k) program. They must provide employees with a ninety-day decision period during which an employee can opt out and get a full, immediate refund of any contribution made during the first three months.

> *"Research has shown that the automated process creates a 'positive presumption' in favor of saving."*

Research has shown that the automated process creates a "positive presumption" in favor of saving. That's exactly what it was supposed to do, and any financial professional could have predicted that because that's what happens when you remove emotions from financial decisions. However, emotions still make people hesitate. Before enrolling and deciding how much to contribute, most people want to get a feel for how much of their salary they'll receive each month. After all, taxes, Social Security, insurance, and other deductions have an impact. Once people receive their first check, though, they'll likely feel there's no way they can afford to contribute a single dime—at least that's what their emotions will tell them.

How can you break free from the emotional decision? It's simple. Don't go out of your way to undo the automatic enrollment. It's the first step in the process of becoming the owner of your PCM Co. and creating paychecks for life. Stick with it.

10-1-NOW Revisited

Now that you understand automatic enrollment, you're probably wondering how much you should contribute. The first thing you should know is that all automatic enrollments come with a default deduction percentage that is usually on the low end—say, 3%. Any 401(k) plan that defaults employees' contributions at the low rate of 3% should have the following warning label: "By defaulting you into our 401(k) plan at the lowest rate allowed by law, we're guaranteeing that you'll fail to create paychecks for life."

> *"By defaulting you into our 401(k) plan at the lowest rate allowed by law, we're guaranteeing that you'll fail to create paychecks for life."*

OPM Revisited

Another reason you do not want to be lulled into contributing the minimum of 3% is that your employer may invest in your PCM Co. as well. The summary plan description of your 401(k) will tell you how much your employer will invest in your PCM Co. via a matching contribution. If your employer wants to contribute 50% of your contribution up to 6% of your pay (a standard), and you're automatically enrolled at 3%, you'd receive only half of the YEM (Your Employer's Money) that you're entitled to.

Your fellow workers may tell you the default rate is 3% and that that's all you should contribute. Don't listen to them.

The Catch-Up Provision

Contribution limits apply regardless of the percentages allowed by any 401(k) plan. As of 2010, you can contribute 100% of your pay up to $16,500. If you're over age fifty, you can contribute another $5,500, for a total of $22,000. This is known as the catch-up provision. The government allows this extra annual contribution because it realizes that Social Security probably won't be around long enough or have enough funds to provide for everyone's retirement, and that most people fifty years of age and older need to catch up on their savings. This is just another glaring reminder to younger folks aged forty-nine and below of why saving 10% now really pays off and lets you avoid playing catch-up later.

2. Auto Placement

What will your company do with the money you contribute? That, of course, is entirely up to you. It's 100% your business; however, if you don't elect where your money and OPM are invested, the automatic placement process will choose a default investment for you. While that may seem risky, the *Employee Retirement Income Security Act* (ERISA) stipulates that the plan sponsor has a fiduciary responsibility to make prudent selections—such as in safe harbors.

Safe Harbors

Current regulations provide for funds called safe harbors, which mean that corporations cannot be sued for breach of fiduciary duty related to the performance of the investments they select. In other words, your company is not responsible if the safe-harbor funds perform poorly even though it selected the funds for you. This does not, however, preclude those fiduciaries from acting in the best interest of you and your fellow 401(k) participants by selecting safe-harbor investments that are prudent choices and monitoring the performance and expenses of these investments. This includes replacing any fund that's underperforming or not in the best interest of you and your fellow workers. The safe harbors are deemed qualified, practical selections for the purpose of retirement funds. We'll discuss safe harbors in more detail under Principle #6 (page 103).

3. Auto Escalation: 10–1–NOW On Auto Pilot

As mentioned previously, if you're automatically enrolled into a 401(k) plan and do not specify a percentage to contribute, one will be selected for you, usually on the low end of the scale, say 3%. However, regardless of the initial percentage contributed, many plans offer automatic escalation. With this feature, your contribution percentage is increased by 1% each year until you reach the 10% maximum.

If you cannot immediately contribute 10% of your pay, the benefit of automatic escalation cannot be overstated. We discussed the concept of marginal thinking in Principle #1, and of compound interest and the benefit of increasing your contribution by 1% per year in Principle #4 (see page 67). Automatic escalation is marginal thinking and 10–1–NOW on autopilot. With automatic escalation, you'll hardly notice the small, increased deductions from your pay each year, thus minimizing the feeling that you don't have enough money to meet your current expenses. Your budget will quickly adjust, but the effect on your PCM Co. will be enormous.

> *"Automatic escalation . . . is marginal thinking and 10–1–NOW on autopilot."*

As with automatic enrollment, waiting for the right time to increase your contribution percentage is not a good idea. That decision involves emotions and, chances are, you'll never find the right time to implement the increase. Reasons not to increase, however, will be plentiful.

4. Auto Rebalancing

Of all the automatic features available to you, automatic rebalancing is perhaps the most difficult, psychologically, for investors to understand.

When you begin investing your capital and OPM into your PCM Co., you should be investing in a diversified portfolio that, over time, will provide you the expected 5% to 7% needs-based rate of return to pay off your desirement mortgage by the time you reach your desirement years. Your investments should be allocated across different investment classes in different percentages to reduce your overall risk (see Principle #6 for more on this). Over time, however, some investments will outperform others, and your asset allocation will stray from your original diversification strategy.

One significant way to reduce this straying effect is to rebalance your portfolio. How does this work? Well, let's say you started with an asset allocation strategy of 50% stocks and 50% bonds. If stocks do poorly and bonds do better, the value of these assets in your portfolio may move from 50/50 to, say, 40/60. You now have a greater percentage of your assets in bonds than you initially wanted. This may, over the long term, reduce your returns if bonds underperform equities. The opposite could also be true. Over a long period of time, equities may perform better than bonds, as was the case in the 1990s, but from 2000 to 2002 the S&P 500 dropped 43%. If your portfolio had become overweighted with a high percentage of stock—say, 90%—and a small percentage of bonds—10%—and then the market dropped 43%, you would have experienced the tragic impact of not having rebalanced.

I liken rebalancing to playing black jack at a casino. Remember that time when the table you were playing got hot and you couldn't stop winning? Now remember what happened when you didn't stop playing and the table (or dealer) turned on you. The losses came strong and hard and maybe even wiped you out. One sure way to leave the casino with more chips than you started with is to periodically take chips off the winning table and move to another one. You also need to put some of those winnings in your pocket throughout the night, until eventually you walk out with more than you started with.

This is true with investing. You may be thinking, "If that investment sector is doing so well, why should I sell when I'm making money?"

The answer is twofold: 1) Eventually all markets turn, and when they do, they turn hard and fast; and 2) You're drifting away from the original guideposts you started investing with. If more and more of your capital ends up in one investment class, your risk exposure may increase, or, conversely, your portfolio may not be poised to earn a large enough return to meet your goals.

Buy Low and Sell High

These five words really sum it up. In the rebalancing process, some of the assets within an overachieving investment category are sold and more of the assets in an underachieving investment category are bought to regain the original asset allocation you decided upon. This is the other important effect of automatic rebalancing: to preserve your original asset allocation strategy and keep it aligned with your needs-based rate of return of 5% to 7%.

Reduce Volatility

Another significant benefit of automatic rebalancing over longer periods of time is the reduced volatility in your portfolio. Volatility is the dramatic swings in a specific investment's returns. When you're earning 50% it's a great ride up, but when that same investment comes crashing down and you experience a 50% loss, that's a 100% swing in returns. That's like riding the Incredible Hulk Coaster at Universal's Islands of Adventure in Orlando. Your emotions will run wild and your investment decisions may prove hazardous to your PCM Co.'s financial health. Most studies show that rebalancing a portfolio to an investor's original asset allocation each year helps reduce the portfolio's volatility. No roller coaster rides here, just smooth and steady returns.

The table that follows shows the results of a study by Craig L. Israelsen, Ph.D. Israelsen is an associate professor at Brigham Young University, the principal of Target Date Analytics (www.ontargetindex.com), and the designer of the 7Twelve Portfolio (www.7TwelvePortfolio.com). He has probably done more research on the benefits of automatic rebalancing than anyone I know. Every one of his studies continues to validate its benefits.

The table compares an annually rebalanced seven-asset portfolio to a buy-and-hold seven-asset portfolio during multiple ten-year periods.

Rebalancing Beats Buying and Holding

Ending Portfolio Balance in a 7-Asset Portfolio*	Rebalance 7-Asset Portfolio Annually	Buy & Hold All 7 Assets	Rebalancing Advantage ($)	Rebalancing Advantage (%)
40-Year Period (1970–2009)	532,991	405,696	127,295	31.4%
30-Year Period (1980–2009)	175,699	153,788	21,911	14.2%
20-Year Period (1990–2009)	42,378	36,821	5,557	15.1%
10-Year Period (2000–2009)	16,765	15,734	1,031	6.6%

*7-Asset portfolio is equally-weighted and consists of : Large cap US equity, Small cap US equity, Non-US equity, Real Estate, Commodities, US Bonds, Cash

Source: www.7TwelvePortfolio.com, Craig L. Israelsen. Used with permission.

Each portfolio had $10,000 invested at the beginning of each period and each asset class received one-seventh of the total investment, or $1,428. The table shows the advantage of annual rebalancing over both short and long periods of time. For example, an investor who rebalanced annually from 1970 to 2009 versus an investor who simply bought and held their investment achieved a $127,295 advantage, or a 31.4% greater return.

Take Emotions out of the Equation

When it comes to manual rebalancing, most people take the wait-and-see approach, but that will nearly guarantee they make the wrong decisions. Why? When you see that some of your funds outpaced the market, you're not going to see those as good candidates for sale. It will be painful to entertain the thought. You'll see those funds as the only reason you made money and will view the lower-performing funds as a drag on your success. Your emotions will go against selling some of your high performers to gain exposure to the low performers. Let technology rescue you from these misguided thoughts.

Successful entrepreneurs understand the power of bad emotions and are intelligent enough to take emotions out of the equation when it comes to investing in their businesses. You need to do the same, and automatic rebalancing is the way.

A Word of Caution about Automatic Investing

Automatic 401(k) investing provides enormous benefit. As with any benefit, though, there can be drawbacks, and it's important for you to be aware of the potential pitfalls. The major drawback to any automated process is that it can lure you into a false sense of confidence. Automation can make you complacent. You may feel there's no need to participate in the process because it all appears to be taken care of.

As nice as a fully automated investment process would be, the automatic features discussed require you to be involved in various parts of the process. Autopilot does not replace pilots. Cruise control does not replace drivers. Instead, these features make some parts of the flying and driving processes easier. They're not intended to take over completely.

That's also true for the automatic features available for your PCM Co. As the entrepreneur, you have decisions to make and goals to set.

How much money do you need for retirement? How much must you contribute to reach those goals? What risks are you willing to take and which do you wish to avoid?

Automatic 401(k) features cannot answer these and other important questions. Without answers, you'll be unable to navigate your way safely to your desirement years, just as you can't go to sleep in the back seat of your car because you're using cruise control. Don't think for a moment that these automatic features do everything for you and that you can just sit back, relax, and do nothing. Planning for your desirement years requires you, the entrepreneur, to take an active role. These processes won't automatically bring success, but they'll make some of your most important decisions easier and more consistent, and they'll limit the negative impact of your emotions—and that's an automatic benefit for your paychecks for life plan.

PAYCHECKS FOR LIFE ACTION STEPS

☐ 401(k) plans offer four powerful automation tools to take the emotion out of decision making: automatic enrollment, automatic placement, automatic escalation, and automatic rebalancing.

☐ Automatic enrollment is the first step in your plan to create paychecks for life. Get started today.

☐ Automatic placement chooses an investment allocation strategy for you if you fail to make an election. You can always change the choices made.

☐ Automatic escalation increases your annual contribution by 1% per year. You'll hardly notice the small, increased deductions from your pay each year. However, the long-term benefits are enormous.

☐ Automatic rebalancing keeps you from letting your emotions talk you out of difficult decisions about when to buy and sell shares in your portfolio. It always ensures you'll sell high and buy low, and that's a long-term recipe for success.

☐ Automated tools make your investment job easier, but they do not replace you completely; you still need to be involved in various parts of the process.

Principle #6

Manage Risk by Outsourcing

Company entrepreneurs are visionaries. They see the big picture: a plan, a path, a purpose. They're responsible for making it all come together. That's a lot to expect. How do entrepreneurs manage all of these difficult tasks? They don't. They outsource certain things to highly specialized talent.

You're now the entrepreneur of your Paycheck Manufacturing Company, and you must outsource various parts of the investment process to professionals so you can meet your goal of creating paychecks for life.

In my thirty-one years as a financial advisor and as The 401(k) Coach, I have discovered that there are two types of investors: those who know (or think they know) what they're doing, and those who don't know and don't want to know the details. (See the following page for a humorous take on the second category; if you're in the first, you'll most likely find what I'm about to say overly simplistic; so be it.)

Clueless

Speed Bump

My basic philosophy of investing in your PCM Co. is as follows:

1. Successful investing requires patience that is measured in years, not weeks.
2. Successful investing is boring. It's like watching paint dry. If you want excitement, visit a casino or jump out of an airplane.
3. Successful investing requires diversification, rebalancing, and dollar-cost averaging.
4. Successful investing requires a personal acknowledgement that you don't have the time, tenacity, or talent to do this yourself. You must outsource the investment process to a professional.

As the entrepreneur of your PCM Co. your job is to manage what you can control: your vision, your desirement mortgage value and payments, and your needs-based rate of return. Investment professionals can manage the rest. Fortunately, most company-sponsored 401(k) plans offer professionally managed investment choices that maximize technology to minimize your involvement. You still have to choose among the options, though, so you should understand the ingredients to risk reduction so you can select the investments that are right for you.

Diversification

Once you contribute money to your 401(k), you must find a place to put it. You need a place for your employees (your dollars) to work. You don't want them to sit as cash forever, earning small amounts of interest that expose you to inflation risk.

The first rule of successful investing is to diversify among a broad range of asset classes that behave differently and are in different markets. Mutual funds are a great investment choice for diversification for a variety of reasons. First, a single investment, no matter how small, in one mutual fund allows you to gain control quickly and efficiently of many stocks or bonds. Second, unlike with individual stocks, mutual funds allow you to buy a fractional share (less than one share), which means you can always invest 100% of your money regardless of the fund price.

Mutual funds can be divided into two camps: actively managed funds and passively managed index funds (exchange traded funds [ETFs] are classified as passively managed index funds). An actively managed fund is one in which the fund manager has discretion over the selection of investments (e.g., stocks, bonds, cash, etc.) and how long investments are held. Passively managed index funds or ETFs typically mimic a specific stock or bond market index, which is why they're referred to as index funds. An index fund manager is constrained to holding the same stocks or bonds as the index he or she is attempting to emulate. Passively managed index funds and ETFs tend to have lower expenses and turnover than actively managed funds.

The most useful function of a professional investment advisor is selecting an appropriate asset allocation consistent with your investment needs, circumstances, and preferences. You can choose to use actively managed funds, passively managed index funds, or a combination of the two, depending on what's available in your 401(k) plan. If you prefer one type of fund over another and it's not available in your plan, you should bring this to your company's attention. After all, this is your money. You should have the options you desire.

Asset Classes

For diversification to work, it's essential that your portfolio represent a wide range of investment asset classes. Each mutual fund you hold must complement the others. They should behave differently, be in different markets, and work over different time periods.

Your 401(k) plan likely offers individual funds in the following investment categories:

U.S. stock funds
   Large-cap
   Mid-cap
   Small-cap
Non-U.S. stock funds
   Developed companies
   Emerging markets
Real estate
Resource funds
   Natural resources
   Commodities
U.S. bond funds
   Aggregate bonds
   Inflation-protected bonds
Non-U.S. bond funds
   International bonds
Cash

The recipe for a diversified strategy is simple:

1. Select twelve funds, one from each asset class above.
2. Allocate your investments equally among the twelve categories.
3. Rebalance the twelve funds on a periodic basis.

For a detailed explanation of a twelve-class portfolio, diversification, and asset allocation strategies, go to www.7TwelvePortfolio.com.

Risk Reduction

Greater diversification is key to managing investment risk. Risk can be measured in different ways:

Volatility of return in a portfolio

The typical measure of volatility in an investment portfolio is standard deviation of return, a statistical measure that's often reported alongside the mean (or average) annualized return of an investment. A mutual fund with a high standard deviation of return would be considered a high-risk fund.

Cumulative return

Cumulative return is a measure of how much an investor's actual account balance increased or decreased over a specific period of time.

Frequency of portfolio loss

This definition of risk measures how often an investment account has lost money over a specified time. "Underwater" is a term used to describe an account that has a lower current balance than the starting balance. The table below shows the annual returns of three portfolios: one composed entirely of large-cap U.S. stocks, one composed of 60% large-cap U.S. stocks and 40% U.S. bonds, and the last the 7Twelve Portfolio.

Annual Returns of Three Portfolios, 2000 to 2009

Year	One-Fund Portfolio* 100% Large-cap U.S. Stock (%)	Two-Fund Portfolio** 60% Large-cap U.S. Stock/40% U.S. Bonds (%)	12-Fund Portfolio 7Twelve Portfolio (%)
2000	−9.70	−1.22	6.78
2001	−11.86	−3.79	−1.58
2002	−21.50	−8.85	−0.68
2003	28.16	18.49	27.08
2004	10.69	8.10	17.73
2005	4.86	3.84	12.30
2006	15.80	11.16	15.38
2007	5.12	5.81	11.25
2008	−36.70	−18.66	−24.62
2009	26.32	17.22	24.99

Year	One-Fund Portfolio* 100% Large-cap U.S. Stock (%)	Two-Fund Portfolio** 60% Large-cap U.S. Stock/40% U.S. Bonds (%)	12-Fund Portfolio 7Twelve Portfolio (%)
3-Year Average Annualized Return (2007–2009)	−5.63	0.30	1.58
5-Year Average Annualized Return (2005–2009)	0.41	3.09	6.31
10-Year Average Annualized Return (2000–2009)	−1.00	2.60	7.81
10-Year Standard Deviation of Annual Returns (2000–2009)	20.90	11.63	15.11
10-Year Growth of $10,000	$9,047	$12,921	$21,212

*Using SPY
**Using 60% SPY/40% LAG
Note: Annual rebalancing assumed for two-Fund Portfolio and 12-Fund Portfolio

Source: www.7TwelvePortfolio.com, Craig L. Israelsen. Used with permission.

As you can see, the 7Twelve Portfolio produced a superior result in most individual years, but its average annualized returns beat the less diversified portfolios for all time periods, and its ten-year growth was significantly better.

> *"The biggest mistake most investors make is to look for the highest-performing funds—i.e., the greeds-based rate of return."*

The biggest mistake most investors make is to look for the highest-performing funds—i.e., the greeds-based rate of return. They feel that selecting lower-performing funds only creates a drag on overall performance. This is not necessarily true. We don't know for sure what's going to happen in the business world; see below for the proof. The table is arranged to show the performance ranking of various asset classes. The patchwork quilt effect is evidence of how much the asset classes trade places in the ranking over time.

Market Trends – Annual Returns (12/31/10)

	Annual Returns											Trailing Returns - 12/31/10		
BEST	2000	2001	2002	2003	2004	2005	2006	2007	2008	2009	2010	5 Yrs	10 Yrs	20 Yrs
	22.83%	14.02%	10.27%	48.54%	22.25%	14.02%	26.86%	11.81%	5.24%	37.21%	29.09%	5.80%	8.42%	12.94%
	11.63%	8.42%	-11.42%	47.25%	20.70%	7.05%	23.48%	11.63%	-28.92%	34.47%	26.86%	5.30%	6.33%	10.84%
	7.02%	2.49%	-15.52%	46.03%	18.33%	6.27%	22.25%	7.05%	-31.50%	32.46%	24.50%	4.47%	5.84%	10.09%
	-3.02%	-5.50%	-15.66%	39.17%	16.49%	6.06%	18.37%	6.96%	-33.79%	28.43%	17.94%	3.75%	4.18%	9.46%
	-3.52%	-5.59%	-16.58%	34.35%	14.31%	5.26%	16.65%	5.77%	-36.85%	27.17%	16.71%	3.71%	3.94%	9.12%
	-7.79%	-9.23%	-20.48%	30.03%	14.27%	4.71%	15.46%	3.96%	-37.60%	25.74%	16.10%	3.52%	3.78%	8.33%
	-13.96%	-12.45%	-21.65%	29.89%	11.40%	4.55%	13.35%	-0.17%	-38.44%	20.58%	15.51%	2.94%	3.26%	8.19%
	-22.43%	-20.42%	-27.88%	29.75%	6.30%	4.15%	9.07%	-1.57%	-38.54%	19.69%	8.21%	2.59%	1.83%	6.89%
WORST	-22.43%	-21.21%	-30.26%	4.11%	4.34%	2.43%	4.33%	-9.78%	-43.06%	5.93%	6.56%	1.28%	0.02%	6.22%

Intermediate Bond Barclays Capital U.S. Aggregate Bond	Small Cap Value Russell 2000 Value	Large Cap Growth Russell 1000 Growth
Small Cap Blend Russell 2000	Large Cap Value Russell 1000 Value	International Equity MSCI EAFE
Large Cap Blend Russell 1000	Small Cap Growth Russell 2000 Growth	Diversified Portfolio

Used with permission from Zephyr Associates inc.

As the owner of your PCM Co., you need to diversify your risk whenever possible, and that means investing some money into lower-performing funds. Diversification allows you to capture decent returns all of the time rather than experience the extreme alternatives between outstanding and horrible returns.

Naïve Diversification

Now that you understand the idea behind diversification and the power it offers, you must make sure you're not diversifying incorrectly. As with any technique, there's a right way and a wrong way.

New investors often attempt to diversify by choosing many high-performing funds; that's not true diversification. Purchasing many separate yet highly related funds is a technique that academics call naïve diversification. It's an inexperienced attempt to manage risk. While it's better than putting all of your money into a single fund, it reduces risk only slightly.

The proper way to diversify is to put dollars in diverse asset classes. You need some "risk" classes and some "safe" classes. You may, for example, choose high-growth stock funds, emerging market funds, and bond funds. Some of these will be lower-performing funds, but don't let that alarm you; it's part of a smart diversification strategy. It's part of managing unforeseen risk. Different types of funds will provide support when others perform poorly.

You can't look at a calendar and see that a bear market is coming. If you try to diversify into safe assets once the wrath of a bear market has struck, bond prices will be sky-high, your equities will be worth peanuts, and you will have missed the opportunity. The average investor left to his or her own devices and investing ignorance will always sell low and buy high, thus producing the worst possible outcome. Market volatility almost always causes emotions to run high and investors to run for safety and sell at the wrong time.

> *"Diversification is a powerful technique, but don't forget the seemingly counterintuitive actions you must accept to achieve it."*

Diversification is a powerful technique, but don't forget the seemingly counterintuitive actions you must accept to achieve it. It's crucial that you understand and believe in the benefits now.

A final point about diversification: although risk can be mitigated by diversifying, risk is a reflection of constantly evolving business and economic cycles and your personal needs over time. Put simply: risk changes over time. That's why rebalancing is so important.

Automatic Rebalancing

I introduced the concept of automatic rebalancing in Principle #5, but it bears repeating. Rebalancing is the systematic process of reallocating the assets within a portfolio to keep each asset's share of the portfolio in line with predetermined percentages.

You may be thinking, "If stocks are doing better than bonds, what's the problem? Why would I want to sell the asset class that's going up and reinvest my money in the one that's going down?" The answer is evident in the table which shows the best- and worst-performing asset classes in any given year from 2000 to 2009. Eventually, your winners will become your losers. If your winners now represent a higher percentage than you started with, your risk exposure has increased, and when that asset class turns negative you may be poised for big losses and become unable to earn your needs-based rate of return.

Those five magic words once again sum it up: buy low and sell high. Rebalancing is the professional and systematic process that guarantees you're always buying something low with dollars you sold from something high, and that's how you make money investing.

> *"Rebalancing . . . guarantees you're always buying something low with dollars you sold from something high, and that's how you make money investing."*

The last point to be made about rebalancing is it smoothes out the volatility in an investment portfolio. Volatility always drives emotion and emotional investing almost always leads to bad decisions.

Qualified Default Investment Alternatives (QDIAs)

When the government decided to allow corporations that sponsor 401(k) plans to implement automatic enrollment, it had to ensure that the funds—the default investment elections—that employees were automatically enrolled in were managed in a prudent way. Default investments do not just apply to first-time enrollments. An increasing number of 401(k) participants actively choose default investments throughout their employment. Others may roll 401(k) plans over from other companies and, likewise, choose default investments.

These default investments aren't just temporary places to invest money until you find something better. They're meant to be qualified selections under *ERISA (Employee Retirement Income Security Act)*. These investment choices fall under the acronym Qualified Default Investment Alternatives, or QDIAs, and they're beneficial for both you the employee and the employer who sponsors your 401(k) plan. QDIAs are also called "safe harbors."

The Department of Labor (DOL) defines a QDIA as an investment fund or model portfolio that's designed to provide both long-term appreciation and capital preservation through a mix of equity and fixed income exposures. Management of the portfolio's investments must be based on an employee's age or their target retirement date. Investment funds or products lacking either a fixed income or an equity exposure generally can't qualify as QDIAs.

There are a variety of investments that can qualify as your 401(k) plan's QDIA: balanced funds, lifestyle funds, life-cycle funds, and target date funds. I'm going to focus exclusively on target date funds because they provide the greatest degree of asset diversification and automatic features for reducing risk exposure by "squirreling" money into less risky asset classes, as you get closer to your desirement years.

Target Date Fund DNA
Target date funds have what I call a particular DNA. They are genetically engineered to reduce their exposure to risky asset classes (e.g., equities, real estate, commodities) over time and increase their exposure to more conservative asset classes (bonds, cash).

The DNA comes in two forms: "glide to" and "glide through" a specific retirement target date.

Target Date Fund DNA

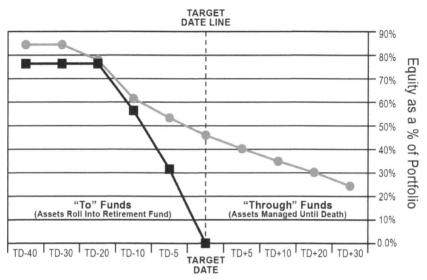

Source: www.7TwelvePortfolio.com, Craig L. Israelsen. Used with permission.

Glide-through target date funds

Target date funds that manage their portfolios based on a glide-through retirement approach use an asset allocation formula that maintains a higher exposure to equities through to an individual investor's life expectancy. The theory is that at age sixty-five, investors will not withdraw 100% of their funds to live on but will continue to invest through to their life expectancy, and, therefore, need to continue to have 50% to 60% of their portfolio in equities to keep pace with taxes and inflation.

Glide-to target date funds

A glide-to target date fund tracks my three phases of investing (see page 34) by taking greater risk in the earning years and reducing risk exposure in the squirreling years (ages fifty-five to sixty-four) by transferring a larger portion of the fund into safer bond and cash equivalent asset classes; by the time you reach your desirement years, 80% to 100% of your investments will be in these safer classes.

So which target date fund is right for you? While everyone's risk tolerance and circumstances are different, I am of the opinion that for the average 401(k) investor, a glide-to target date fund is the way to go. As you get closer to your desirement date, the impact of a negative (bear) market could be devastating, as many investors realized in 2008.

The following table shows this clearly. The table compares three different investments. The performance of a glide-through target date fund is represented by the Fidelity Freedom 2010 Target Fund. As of this writing, this fund encompassed approximately 50% of all the money invested in target date funds. The Fidelity Balanced Fund invests approximately 50% in equities and 50% in bonds or cash at all times. The 7Twelve Life Stage Portfolio is a glide-to target date fund, reducing its exposure to equity classes as it got closer to 2010.

The investment period is 2000 to 2009, and each fund had $10,000 invested at the beginning of 2000. This ten-year period also represented one of the worst ten-year periods of all time for investors, with two of the worst bear markets since the Great Depression.

The 7Twelve fund had positive returns for the three-, five-, and ten-year periods, with an average annual return of 7.30% versus the Fidelity Freedom fund's 2.73% This represented almost a $7,000 gain for the 7Twelve over the Fidelity Freedom fund. In 2002, when the Fidelity Freedom and Fidelity Balanced funds had –6.85% and –8.50% returns, respectively, the 7Tweleve had a positive 1.26%. In 2008, when the equity markets suffered their worst losses since the Great Depression, the Fidelity Freedom fund was down –25.32% and the Fidelity Balance fund was –31.31%. Compare that to the 7Twelve, which had about half the loss, or –14.32%

Protecting your hard-earned money prior to your desirement years is an important goal. A properly designed target date fund with a glide-to DNA can do this for you.

Glide-To Beats Glide-Through: 2010 Target Date Funds

Year	Investor Age	Fidelity Freedom 2010 Target Fund (FFFCX) (%)	Fidelity Balanced (FBLAX) (%)	7Twelve Life Stage Portfolios* (%)
2000	55	0.67	5.32	7.35
2001	56	−4.34	2.25	−0.08
2002	57	−6.85	−8.50	1.26
2003	58	17.13	28.24	22.57
2004	59	7.28	10.94	15.13
2005	60	5.92	10.68	8.49
2006	61	9.46	11.65	10.26
2007	62	7.43	8.99	10.17
2008	63	−25.32	−31.31	−14.32
2009	64	24.82	28.05	16.89
3-Year Average Annualized Return		**0.04**	**−1.40**	**3.33**
5-Year Average Annualized Return		**3.03**	**3.45**	**5.71**
10-Year Average Annualized Return		**2.73**	**5.20**	**7.30**
10-Year Growth of $10,000		**$13,087**	**$16,607**	**$20,230**

*7Twelve Life Stage 50 to 60 Portfolio from age 55–59; 7Twelve Life Stage 60–70 Portfolio from ages 60 to 64.

Source: *7Twelve: A Diversified Investment Portfolio with a Plan*, Craig L. Israelsen (Wiley, 2010). Used with permission

Here is a short list of target date funds (which would qualify as QDIAs in your 401(k) plan) worth considering. Be certain you understand the glide-path DNA of each and choose the one that fits your long-term risk tolerance and desirement mortgage planning.

Glide-Through Retirement DNA:

- Fidelity Freedom Fund: www.fidelity.com
- Nationwide Destination Funds: www.nationwide.com
- T. Rowe Price Retirement: www.troweprice.com
- Vanguard Target Retirement: www.vanguard.com

Glide-To Retirement DNA:

- American Century Livestrong: www.americancentury.com
- MFS Life Time: www.mfs.com
- Stadion Target Date: www.stadionmoney.com
- WellsFargo Advantage Dow Jones Target: www.wellsfargo.com

The bottom line: outsource. Remember, you're the entrepreneur. You're not expected to know everything but you're expected to make rational decisions when it comes to managing your company. Don't feel you're doing yourself a disservice by outsourcing if you're not comfortable with finance and investing. Instead, realize you're making the decision to hire a professional manager for your PCM Co.—every successful entrepreneur knows he or she can't do it alone.

QDIAs allow you, the entrepreneur, to outsource asset allocation decisions to an investment professional. They prevent your emotions from getting in the way. Most importantly, they provide for better returns over time. Don't think they're second-rate selections. If you now understand why chasing performance is a bad idea, you'll understand one of the many reasons why QDIAs are beneficial. Choose those with the correct glide-to DNA that will most likely glide you into your desirement years safely.

PAYCHECKS FOR LIFE ACTION STEPS

☐ Remember successful investing requires patience. It should be as exciting as watching paint dry.

☐ Use diversification, dollar cost averaging, and automatic rebalancing to reduce your investment risk and achieve your needs-based rate of return.

☐ Outsource the design of your investment portfolio to professionals, and don't let your emotions get in the way.

☐ Select a target date fund with a glide-to DNA. It will automatically reduce your risk over time and help you squirrel away and protect your PCM Co. assets as you approach your desirement years.

☐ As of this writing, there were 40 different mutual fund companies with 400 distinct target date funds holding nearly $400 billion in retirement plan assets. Brightscope (www.brightscope.com) and Target Date Analytics, LLC (www.ontargetindex.com) are two independent firms who have joined forces to provide a comprehensive analysis of target date fund families called "Popping the Hood."

Principle #7:

Control Fees and Expenses

As entrepreneur of your PCM Co., you have many important decisions to make, decisions that will fall into two basic categories. First, you must decide on how to make money. Second, and equally important, you must figure out how to control costs. After all, it's not what you make that counts; it's what you keep. Reducing expenses is identical to making profits.

The majority of 401(k) participants are not aware of all the costs involved in managing their money. Understanding these costs is just as important as building a diversified investment strategy that takes advantage of dollar cost averaging and automatic rebalancing. What's the point of having a great investment strategy if you're paying too much for it?

> *"What's the point of having a great investment strategy if you're paying too much for it?"*

If you were to open your own business today, you'd have to pay a wide variety of expenses. Entrepreneurs call all the expenses a business incurs to keep its door open and to operate successfully their "overhead." Normal company overhead costs can be broken down into two categories: 1) Hard-dollar expenses, including rent, utilities, insurance, legal and accounting services, and other business expenses unrelated to employees; and 2) Soft-dollar expenses for employee-related items like salaries, bonuses, medical insurance, sick leave, and Social Security. Your 401(k) plan also has hard- and soft-dollar expenses.

Hard-Dollar Expenses

Hard-dollar expenses are the fees charged to a 401(k) plan to cover the day-to-day operations of the plan. These expenses are usually not communicated to plan participants. They include the cost of keeping your 401(k) plan in compliance with current *ERISA* and DOL (Department of Labor) regulations. These costs are specifically known as plan administration, design, and compliance expenses.

These hard-dollar fees are typically paid for by your employer. In other words, you do not pay these overhead expenses. Imagine starting a business and your rich Uncle Louie comes along and says, "I'll pay all of the expenses to operate your business with the exception of your employee costs." Not a bad deal.

But there are exceptions to this rule. Some employers pay for these expenses out of the assets of the plan. That is, they're indirectly paid by you and all other plan participants, often without your knowledge. You can find out if this is the case where you work by asking your employer.

Most 401(k) plans also offer individual services such as loan and distribution provisions. Whenever you use these services you will probably have to pay a one-time processing charges of $50 or $100. While these fees usually aren't high, be sure you understand what you'll incur before availing yourself of any individual services.

Soft-Dollar Expenses

Soft-dollar fees cover a wide range of services including record keeping, website services, automated access to your investment information, and customer education and advice services. In addition, costs are associated with managing the money within each mutual fund in your 401(k). These expenses include investment management fees, 12-b1 fees, subtransfer fees, asset-based or wrap fees, and revenue-sharing fees. The total of all these fund expenses represent the expense ratio of the mutual fund. Let's break these expenses down individually.

Fund Expense Fees

Fund expense fees are automatically deducted by the mutual fund company that manages your money. These fees will affect your performance, sometimes significantly, so you must understand how they work and the impact they have.

Mutual funds can be broken down into two basic categories: load funds and no-load funds. Load funds charge up-front expenses that immediately reduce your PCM Co.'s profitability. The front-end load is an acquisition charge that's typically used by the mutual fund company to offset marketing and sales expenses. These expenses can be as high as 5% on every dollar you invest.

In a 401(k), you'll typically never be offered load funds for which you have to pay the load. (If you are, go immediately to those responsible for managing the plan—i.e., the plan's fiduciaries—and demand to be offered no-load funds.) You may, however, be offered load funds inside your 401(k) where the load or front-end expense has been waived by the mutual fund company. This is a good thing, as many excellent mutual fund companies have front-end expenses. Because your plan's fiduciary has negotiated away those expenses on your behalf, you can still have access to these excellent money managers.

No-load funds charge no front-end or acquisition charges and no back-end surrender charges. You're free to move your money from fund to fund without being charged. Think of it like driving down an interstate and going through a tollbooth that doesn't charge for using the highway.

Investment management fees

These are the fees charged by a mutual fund company to pay for the investment managers who manage your assets. The fees are charged as a percentage of the assets invested (such as 0.25% to 2%) and deducted from the investment returns.

12-b1 fees
These are distribution expenses paid by mutual funds from fund assets. They include broker commissions, marketing expenses, and other administrative costs. The fees may range from 0.25% to 1.25% of assets invested.

Sub-transfer fees
Brokerage firms and mutual funds often contract record keeping and other services related to participant shares to a third party called a sub-transfer agent. The fee can be paid as a fixed fee on a per participant basis, an asset-based fee, or a combination of both. It usually is about 0.05% of assets invested in a mutual fund.

Asset-based or wrap fees
This is an additional fee levied by the plan provider who operates your 401(k) record keeping system. The fee covers additional overhead and expenses not covered by other charges. Often this additional expense is not disclosed to plan participants. Your employer should know this cost so be sure to ask, as it typically is deducted from plan assets and reduces your investment return.

Revenue-sharing fees
The mutual funds in your 401(k) plan may pay a revenue-sharing fee to the company that operates the plan. The payment covers some portion of the management fees associated with record keeping and other services provided to your company's 401(k) plan.

I liken revenue-sharing to slotting fees in the supermarket business. Go to the main supermarket in your town and walk down the breakfast cereal aisle. Count the number of cereal boxes available to your children. There are hundreds. Do your kids (and you) need that many sugared cereals to choose from? No. Why are they all there? Because the supermarket chains benefit from them being there. They may charge a breakfast cereal company $250,000 to slot (or place) its box of cereal on the shelf. This is also known as a placement fee. Cereal companies pay big money to get their boxes in the best place on the shelf. When the supermarket sells that box of cereal it might earn a margin of only three cents; the real money is in the slotting or placement fees.

Your 401(k) provider's platform (think Fidelity, Nationwide, etc.) is a supermarket shelf of mutual funds. Each of the mutual funds, like the cereal company, is looking for the best placement on the shelf. They pay a slotting fee for that privilege, and this is what the industry calls revenue sharing. (Incidentally, if you understand this, you probably now know more than your employer does about the hidden fees associated with your 401(k) plan.)

Plan consulting fees

These are the fees paid to a registered investment advisor, or consultant, or they can be commissions paid to a broker for the advisory services he or she provides to your company's 401(k) plan. They may be paid directly by your employer as a hard-dollar expense or indirectly by you and all the employees in the plan as a soft-dollar expense, which is deducted from the investment assets in each fund.

Basis Points and Expense Ratios

Each of the above fund fees will most likely be reported in *basis points* (often abbreviated "bp"), where one basis point equals one-one hundredth of 1% (i.e., one hundred basis points = 1%). A basis point just identifies all digits to the right hand side of the decimal in a percentage amount: if interest rates increase from 10% to 10.25%, they have increased by twenty-five basis points.

Why bother with basis points and not just stick with percentages? The financial industry uses them to avoid uncertainty. For example, if interest rates are 10% and are reported to have increased by 1%, you may be uncertain if they moved to 10.1% (a 1% relative increase) or 11% (an absolute gain of 1%). It's much clearer to use basis points. If interest rates of 10% are reported to have increased by ten basis points, there's no question they're now 10.1%.

The figure on the following page shows how all of these fees can be paid.

Fees

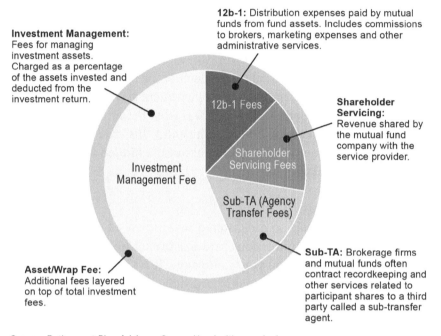

Source: Retirement Plan Advisory Group. Used with permission.

The Securities and Exchange Commission (SEC) requires all funds to disclose both shareholder fees and operating expenses in a fund prospectus, a legal document you should receive for each fund in which you invest, and which you can access at any time from your company's 401(k) plan. The prospectus provides material information about investment objectives, performance, risk, manager tenure, and more. In addition, your 401(k) website should have a simplified fund fact sheet for each investment, which will summarize all fund expenses.

In addition, the DOL has announced sweeping new regulations for participant fee disclosure under *ERISA* 404(a)(5). Under this new regulation, all 401(k) providers must disclose to you on your quarterly statement, in plain English, the amount of money that has been deducted each quarter from your investment account. Look for these changes on your 401(k) investment statement beginning in November 2012.

Not All Fees Are Created Equal

Bonds vs. Stocks

In most cases, a given charge will be lower relative to a fund's return for a stock fund than a bond fund. For example, if a stock fund charges one hundred basis points (1%) and returns 10% for the year, the relative cost to you is 10% (1% / 10%) of your returns.

Bond funds, on the other hand, because of the lower risk, are expected to have lower returns. If a bond fund charges the same one hundred basis points but returns 5%, the relative cost to you is 20% (1% / 5%). Not only do you need to pay attention to the absolute cost (1% in this example), but also the relative costs (10% and 20% respectively). Not all basis points are created equally; you must consider them against the expected returns.

Active vs. Passive Management

Fees will also vary based on whether the fund is actively or passively managed.

Actively managed funds employ fund managers and research staffs who monitor performance. They constantly watch economic data and market valuations to determine whether they should buy, sell, or hold positions. Their goal, of course, is to outperform broad-based indexes such as the S&P 500. Due to the additional time, staffing, and associated trading costs, actively managed funds will have higher fees than their passively managed counterparts.

Passively managed accounts are run on autopilot, so there's no need for managers and research staffs. They're usually tied to an index, such as the S&P 500, which is easy to do. The fund simply buys the same securities in the same proportions as the index and then holds on. The fund mirrors the index and rises and falls with it, dollar for dollar. There's no daily monitoring, research, or heavy trading activity, so the fees tend to be significantly lower.

For passive funds, expense ratios may range from 10 to 25 bp (basis points) and for active funds, 65 to 250 bp.

Large vs. Small Funds

Another factor that drives a fund's expense ratio is the fund size. As a general rule, smaller funds and specialized funds (emerging markets or

Internet technology, for example) are more expensive to operate; therefore, their expense ratios will be higher. However, the average expense ratio for the top funds (in terms of total assets managed) stands at about 73 bp (0.73%).

It's important to note that fund performance is always calculated after the expense ratio. If your fund earned 10% last year and had a one-hundred-basis-point (1%) expense ratio, the performance would be listed at 9%. That number is what you'll see published in the prospectuses and websites that track mutual fund performances.

Retail vs. Institutional Funds

Another distinction between different types of mutual funds—that of retail vs. institutional—also impacts your fund expense fees. Retail funds are available to any consumer. You can buy them directly from a mutual fund company outside your 401(k) or you can select them inside your plan. Although in both cases you're usually buying the same fund with the same professional money manager, the underlying fund expenses may be lower when purchasing inside your 401(k). The reason for this is something called "share class." You can think of this like the ancient feudal system, where the aristocracy enjoyed the benefits of the land at no cost while the upper class and especially the lowest class paid more, if allowed, for the same privileges. The larger the 401(k) plan you're a member of (in terms of its total assets), the greater the negotiating power the plan's fiduciaries have in getting the share class of mutual funds with the lowest expenses.

Institutional funds, on the other hand, are not available to the average consumer. By "average" I mean someone who is looking to invest 10% of their pay or up to the maximum allowable contribution of $22,000 per year ($16,500 plus the $5,500 catch-up provision, if eligible).

Large 401(k) providers—those with billions of dollars under management—will go directly to professional money managers who specialize in wealthy clients who invest $5 million or more at a time (a far cry from your 10% or $22,000). They'll hire these managers to build a fund or manage money in a particular investment asset class—say, emerging markets—for their 401(k) plans. This is known as an institutional fund. You can't buy it directly yourself, but you can access it in your 401(k) plan. This is a great benefit, because your company's 401(k) plan just elevated you from lower to aristocratic status and provided you access to the best professional money management. The fees for institutional funds will be historically lower than the fees for comparable retail funds.

What Impact Do Fees Have on Your Paychecks for Life?

Mutual fund fees can be deceptive. As consumers, we're used to dealing with large percentages. We may leave a 20% tip for excellent service and expect to see 30% off or more for a good department store sale. Therefore, when we see numbers like one-half of 1% (fifty basis points) applied to mutual fund expenses, they sound small, almost insignificant. Nevertheless, as an entrepreneur, you must always remember this important point: expenses compound over time. Though compounding works for you when it comes to your returns, it works against you with expenses. Remember our discussion about marginal thinking in Principle #1? Little amounts over long periods of time make a significant difference inside your PCM Co. You must track expenses meticulously and understand how they affect performance, because they're every bit as meaningful as returns. A dollar saved is a dollar earned.

> *"You must track expenses meticulously and understand how they affect performance, because they're every bit as meaningful as returns. A dollar saved is a dollar earned."*

The following table demonstrates the impact of fees on long-term performance. Three PCM Co. entrepreneurs—Susan, George, and Morgan—all save $10,000 per year. Each earns 7% per year on his or her investment. Over long periods of time, a .50% savings can equal $100,000 or more in real money saved.

The Impact of Fees

Savings Rate: $10,000

Average Rate of Return: 7%

Expense Fee 0.5% - Susan, 1.00% - George, 1.50% - Morgan

Year	Savings	Fee #1 Susan Fee	Fee #1 Susan Balance	Savings	Fee #2 George Fee	Fee #2 George Balance	Loss to Fee #1	Savings	Fee #3 Morgan Fee	Fee #3 Morgan Balance	Loss to Fee #1	Loss to Fee #2
			$50,000			$50,000				$50,000		
1	$10,000	$321	$63,879	$10,000	$642	$63,558	-$321	$10,000	$963	$63,237	-$642	-$321
5	$10,000	$648	$128,967	$10,000	$1,276	$126,321	-$2,646	$10,000	$1,884	$123,722	-$5,245	-$2,599
10	$10,000	$1,191	$236,981	$10,000	$2,304	$228,119	-$8,862	$10,000	$3,344	$219,596	-$17,385	-$8,523
15	$10,000	$1,933	$384,726	$10,000	$3,676	$363,898	-$20,828	$10,000	$5,243	$344,276	-$40,450	-$19,622
20	$10,000	$2,949	$586,817	$10,000	$5,505	$545,002	-$41,815	$10,000	$7,712	$506,419	-$80,398	-$38,583
25	$10,000	$4,338	$863,245	$10,000	$7,945	$786,561	-$76,684	$10,000	$10,923	$717,281	-$145,964	-$69,281
30	$10,000	$6,238	$1,241,354	$10,000	$11,200	$1,108,756	-$132,598	$10,000	$15,099	$991,500	-$249,853	-$117,256

It's not my intention to say that mutual funds should operate for free and allow you to get all the benefits for nothing. Instead, my aim is to show how a small change in fees can make a big impact on the value of your PCM Co. Expenses, as small as they may seem, really do matter. While you'll never find a fund with no fees, you do have the ability to choose among many funds, and this is where you must think like an entrepreneur. If you find two funds that are similar in their investment objectives and historical performance, be sure to check expense ratios and consider them carefully before investing.

Are Higher Fees Worth the Price?

Now that you understand the impact of mutual fund expenses on your investment performance, I'm sure many of you are wondering if there's ever a time when it's beneficial to pay the higher fees. If two funds are similar but one has a long-term track record of 14% returns while the other returns 10%, is it worth it to pay another fifty or one hundred basis points for the higher-performing fund?

Before I answer that, let's be clear about fund performance. Remember that past performance is no guarantee of future performance. Just because one fund had higher returns doesn't mean it will continue to do so. At a minimum, be sure you're looking at long-term performance—say ten years or more—before making comparisons. While that still doesn't provide any guarantee that a fund will continue to be the better performer, it's infinitely better than making comparisons by considering only last year's numbers.

That said, let's now understand some of the basic math that will help you to make decisions. As a rule of thumb, expenses can just be subtracted from expected gains in order to make comparisons. For instance, a 10% fund charging a 1% fee is effectively earning about 9% (10% – 1%). Keeping that in mind, let's assume you're comparing two similar funds. One has a ten-year track record of 10% returns and charges 1%, while the other has returned 14% over the same time period but charges 1.5%. Is it worth it to pay the fifty extra basis points for the 14% fund?

To put the funds on a level playing field, we can subtract the fees from each and then make comparisons. The first fund is effectively returning 9% (10% − 1%). The second is returning 12.5% (14% − 1.5%). The second fund is, therefore, better by about 3.5% (12.5% − 9%). Assuming you believe the second fund will continue to outperform the first by at least 0.5% (the difference in their expense ratios), you're better off going with it. The higher fees are justified by the performance.

Now, for all the mathematicians out there, I know these numbers aren't perfect. They're intended to be used as a rule of thumb. If you want to get exact comparisons, we can do that with a little mathematical trick. Any full price can be multiplied by one minus a discount rate to get the discounted price. For instance, if the full price of something is $50 and it's 20% off, the discounted price is $40 ($50 × [1 − 0.2]).

We can use that same technique to compare the net return of mutual funds. In the previous example, the 10% fund had a 1% expense ratio. The expenses reduce your return by a factor of 0.99 (1 − 0.01). The effective return of that fund is, therefore, 8.9% (0.10 × 0.99). In other words, a fund returning a flat 8.9% per year (i.e., no expenses) is identical to a fund returning 10% with 1% expenses.

In that same example, the 14% fund had a 1.5% expense ratio. A 1.5% deduction is the same as multiplying by 0.985 (1 − 0.015). Therefore, that fund is effectively returning 12.29% (0.14 × 0.985).

Now that we've accounted for the different expenses, we can make direct comparisons in performance. The difference between the two funds is 3.39% (12.29% − 8.9%), which is pretty close to the 3.5% estimate we arrived at earlier—without all the fuss.

If you're torn between two similar funds with different expense ratios, my best advice is this: subtract the expense ratio from the performance of each fund and then compare the results. Invest in the fund that has the highest effective return. Whatever you do, don't get too wrapped up into finding the "best" one. Remember, next year's numbers are going to be different regardless of the historical track record.

The mutual funds you have to select from in your 401(k) will be more than adequate to produce paychecks for life. As we discussed in the previous chapter, a target date fund with the correct DNA for you—i.e., one that glides to your desirement years—will automate the diversification and rebalancing processes for you. If your plan offers more than one target date fund family, look closely at their glide paths—their long-term performance, management tenure, and total expenses. Pick the target date fund with the right DNA for you, the longest history of high performance, a money manager whose tenure is as long as the historical performance period (so you know you're working with the same professionals who produced that result), and the lowest reasonable fees. Then select only one target date fund. Often I see 401(k) investors choose two or three target date funds because they believe this gives them greater diversification. One target date fund is typically made up of twelve different asset classes.

The most important point for you to gain from this chapter is that expenses count. Remember, it's not what you make, it's what you keep that matters. While fund fees appear small as a percentage, they compound over time and dilute your returns. As the entrepreneur, it's your job to pay close attention to the fees and understand the impact they have. Once you do, you won't be fooled by their small size. As Benjamin Franklin once said, "Beware of little expenses. A small leak will sink a great ship."

PAYCHECKS FOR LIFE ACTION STEPS

☐ Fund expense fees are automatically deducted by the mutual fund company.

☐ A fund's expense ratio shows the fund's entire annual operating expenses as a percentage of the fund's average net assets. This is the key figure to watch—relative to a fund's performance—when making comparisons among funds.

☐ Mutual fund fees compound over time. The same advantages you gain from compounding work against you for expenses.

☐ If you're torn between two similar funds with different expense ratios, subtract the expense ratio from the performance of each fund and compare the results.

☐ For a really cool calculator to track and compare fees in mutual fund investments go to www.finra.org/Investors/index.htm. FINRA is the Financial Industry Regulatory Authority. Click on Tools & Calculators, then go to their Fund Analyzer page. Fund Analyzer offers information and analysis on over 18,000 mutual funds and ETFs. This tool estimates the value of the fund and the impact of fees and expenses on your investments.

Principle #8

Guarantee Your Paychecks for Life with Annuities

"Show me the money!"

This line, shouted by Rod Tidwell to Jerry Maguire during an intense phone call in the hit movie *Jerry Maguire*, has become a classic phrase that highlights the heart of business negotiations. When it comes to making deals, it all comes down to one thing—the money.

Up to this point, I've shown you how to begin building your PCM Co. I've shown many principles and practices that center on mechanics, decision making, time, and money. But now it's my turn to listen to you. And I already know what you're saying: "Show me the money!"

It's a valid request. You've built a fabulous business worth hundreds of thousands, perhaps millions, of dollars, but how does that translate into paychecks for life? It can't be as simple as spending the money you've saved, can it? Not at all. It's possible your account could lose value or that you live longer than expected. So how can I be sure you'll generate not just paychecks for life, but, more importantly, guaranteed paychecks for life by following this system? Because I'm advising you to take one last important entrepreneurial step, and that's to insure your success. It's what Linda and Jerry Stevens, our millionaires next door, chose to do, and it's the reason they sat in my office so calmly and contentedly that wintry day in December 2008 while the global credit crisis was freezing markets all over the world and turning most people's 401(k)s into 201(k)s.

Most people in 2008 (and 2009) were feeling like the couple below.

Our Nest Egg Is Being Recalled, Too

Source: Joel Pett Editorial Cartoon used with the permission of Joel Pett and the Cartoonist Group. All rights reserved.

But not Jerry and Linda. Why? Because they had chosen to transfer a percentage of their 401(k) account balances into an annuity product that would guarantee them a specific return on their investments and a guaranteed income for life.

Earlier, I laid out the three phases of investing:

The Three Phases of Investing

Earning years	Squirreling years	Desirement years
Accumulate	Protect	Spend
Ages 21 to 54	Ages 55 to 64	Ages 65 to life expectancy

Once you have accumulated enough money in your PCM Co. in your earning years and have passed into your squirreling years, you face different risks. You need to protect the capital you have accumulated and make sure it generates paychecks for life that will allow you to maintain your lifestyle (i.e., pay for your desirements). That's a tall order for any entrepreneur to manage. How do you do it?

Avoid Excess Withdrawal

Making the money you have accumulated in your PCM Co. last for the duration of your desirement years is something you must master. Drawing down the investments in your PCM Co. too quickly, regardless of how well your diversified portfolio is balanced, puts you at risk of running out of money. In theory, 4% is regarded as a sustainable rate of withdrawal each year to cover one's expenses. In practice, that number could be higher or lower depending on your age, health, and other factors, such as how your investments are allocated through your desirement years.

The next table shows how the withdrawal amount and portfolio allocation can affect the probability that you'll be able to meet your income needs over a twenty-five-year desirement period. It assumes withdrawals of an inflation-adjusted percentage of the initial portfolio value each year beginning in year one. The chance of a portfolio lasting over the desirement period is more likely as the amount withdrawn decreases.

Probability of Meeting Income Needs

83%	97%	96%	94%	92%	4% Withdrawal rate
30%	72%	82%	83%	82%	5%
3%	29%	57%	66%	69%	6%
0%	6%	30%	47%	54%	7%
0%	0%	13%	31%	41%	8%
100% Bonds	75% B 25% S	50% B 50% S	25% B 75% S	100% Stocks	

Source: Morningstar, used with permission

What this table illustrates is the sustainability of an investment portfolio during someone's desirement years—or the potential for ruination. What it does not show is the impact of entering your desirement years in a bear or negative market, as the Stevens's appeared to be headed. If you were to start drawing out paychecks for life from your PCM Co. and experienced negative returns in your investment portfolio during the first few years, your chances of outliving your income increase 25% to 35%.

In an article entitled "Retirement Ruin and the Sequencing of Returns," authors Moshe A. Milevsky and Anna Abaimova demonstrate, with empirical evidence, that a negative return in the first year of retirement could be the difference of fourteen more years of lost paychecks for life. The table below assumes someone withdraws $750 monthly from a $100,000 portfolio—$9,000 per year. It shows the hypothetical sequence of returns in three-year incremental cycles until the money runs out; i.e., what the authors call the "ruin age."

The Retirement Merry-Go-Round

What stop did you get on the retirement merry-go-round?		
Return Sequence	Ruin Age	+/– Months
+7%, +7%, +7% . . .	86.50	
+7%, –13%, +27% . . .	83.33	–38
+7%, +27%, –13% . . .	89.50	+36
–13%, +7%, +27% . . .	81.08	–65
+27%, +7%, –13% . . .	94.92	+101

*Assumes $9,000 spending per year.

Source: *Pensionize™ Your Nest Egg: How to Use Product Allocation to Create a Guaranteed Income for Life,* Moshe A. Milevsky & Alexandra C. Macqueen (Wiley, 2010). Used with permission.

The first return sequence is for a constant 7% annual return. All other return sequences are for an average return of 7%, which can be produced in multiple ways. For example, the second sequence of returns in the table shows an investor earning 7% the first year, –13% the second, and 27% the third. The arithmetic average of these numbers is 7%. In each column marked "Return sequence" the pattern is continued, only the order of the returns changes. Note that if you started taking paychecks from your PCM Co. in the year when your portfolio returns were –13%, your income would last only to age eighty-one, far short of your life expectancy. As Professor Milevsky states, "This is yet another indication of how fragile the first few investment years of withdrawals can really be . . . and why they should be protected. Don't leave your retirement income at the mercy of a spinning merry-go-round."

Convert Your Investments into Annuities: Guaranteed Paychecks for Life

Today, thanks to technology and insurance companies (and their clever actuaries), you can guarantee that your paychecks for life won't expire before you do. You can avoid financial ruin in your desirement years and have greater peace of mind now by transferring 100% of the investment risk and longevity risk to an insurance company.

You already create this peace of mind every day with respect to your home, automobile, health, and even your life. Think about it: do you have fire insurance on your house, auto insurance, health insurance, and life insurance? The premiums you pay the insurance company are the cost of the peace of mind you get in knowing that if your home burns down, the insurance company will give you money to replace it; if your car is damaged in an accident, the insurance company will give you money to repair it; if you get sick or injured and end up in the hospital, your health insurance company will pay your medical bills; and should you die prematurely, the life insurance company will give money to those you love. All of that's what I call peace-of-mind insurance. Shouldn't you consider doing the same thing for the investments in your PCM Co. and your paychecks for life? Imagine protecting them from the risks of a prolonged negative market (bear market) or surpassing your life expectancy (longevity risk).

The life insurance industry will do this for you. In exchange for a small premium or percentage of your investment each year (1%-3%, depending on the features and benefits your purchase) they will:

- protect 100% of the value of your investment;
- increase the value of your investment by a specified rate (5% to 8%) and for a specified period of time (ten to twenty years);
- guarantee to pay out a fixed percentage (5% to 7%) of your investments in the form of an annual income (paycheck) for life;
- offer you the ability to continue to invest in a diversified portfolio (target date funds or investments of your choice) to benefit from the upside gains in the market;
- lock in market gains to increase your potential lifetime income.

In order to guarantee your paychecks for life, you must convert a percentage of your paycheck for life assets (401(k), IRA, and other investments) into a steady stream of guaranteed payments, otherwise called *annuity* payments. You're probably wondering how to do this and how much of your total investments to convert. I'll get to that in a moment. First, let's talk about what annuities are and how they work.

In my financial seminars, I find participants fall into two groups when it comes to annuities. One group has no idea what they are and the other has heard of them but harbors negative views after reading bad press about them. For the latter group, take note: Federal Reserve Chief Ben Bernanke believes in annuities. Bernanke's 2009 financial disclosure, released by the U.S. Office of Government Ethics in July 2010, showed that he had left most of his money where it had been prior to the 2008 economic turmoil, "in no frill annuities. His largest holdings are in two annuities."

Today's annuities are not the same as when your parents and grandparents purchased them. Just as the financial markets have become more flexible and sophisticated, so have annuity products. Let's keep an open mind.

What Is an Annuity?

An annuity is simply a contract between you and an insurance company. As with any contract, the terms can be altered in many ways, but the basic idea is that you, the account holder, make a single payment or a series of payments to the insurance company today in exchange for periodic payments from the insurer in the future.

There are four basic types of annuities: immediate (SPIA), fixed, indexed, and variable.

Single Premium Immediate Annuity (SPIA)

Benefits

An immediate annuity is based on a very simple concept: you make a one-time payment to the insurance company and they immediately agree to begin paying you an income (paycheck) for life—payments that you can never outlive. For example, a sixty-five-year-old man who invests $100,000 in an immediate annuity in 2011 would collect $8,112 per year for the rest of his life. Based on interest rates in 2011, that's about twice as much as he could withdraw safely from his PCM Co.

each year if he followed the widely accepted recommendations to limit withdrawals to 4% of his investment portfolio to avoid outliving his savings.

Immediate annuities offer several important features. First, if you don't have any beneficiaries and are not concerned with leaving any money to anyone, you could take what's called a "life only" option. This means you'll receive the highest monthly payment offered by the insurance company for as long as you live. If you die one month after your first payment, the balance remains with the insurance company—a good deal for them, and a bad deal for no one else, since you weren't leaving the money to anyone to begin with. If, however, you live to be a hundred, a good many years beyond normal life expectancy (which is possible), this would be a good deal for you and a bad deal for the insurance company— and that's what it's all about, the law of averages. The insurance company is betting you'll die too soon, while you're betting you'll live too long. The insurer pools your risk with millions of other policyholders. People who die early end up subsidizing the payment of people who live longer. All the while, you have the peace of mind and financial security of knowing you'll not outlive your income, no matter when you pass away.

Payouts can vary enormously by insurance company, so it's a good idea to compare payouts as well as ratings. A professional insurance advisor can help you with these comparisons. In addition, a variety of payout options are available besides the "life only" option described above. For those of you who want to leave a paycheck for life to your spouse or other family members (such as children), there are many other payment options. These include the "life certain" option, which pays the income over a certain period of time; and the "life and survivor" option, which will determine the percentage of your guaranteed income that will be paid to your spouse upon your death (such as 50% of the income for his or her lifetime). The options affect the amount of income you'll receive over your lifetime, so be sure to make accurate comparisons. This is where a professional financial advisor is worth their weight in gold; they can assist you to determine which choice is best for you and your beneficiaries.

You also want to be certain the insurance company you give your hard-earned PCM Co. assets to today has the financial staying power to continue paying your paychecks for life. Numerous websites provide comparisons of insurance company financial information, including www.ambest.com, www.duffandphelps.com, and www.moodys.com.

Drawbacks

The drawback of an immediate annuity is that you give up complete control over your principal. If you invest $100,000 into an SPIA and a year from now you need some of that money, you're out of luck. All you'll receive are your monthly payments.

Inflation risks

While you buy an SPIA to guarantee you won't outlive your income, the biggest risk you face with this type of product is inflation risk. For example, if your guaranteed monthly income from the SPIA is $2,000, or $24,000 a year, and inflation averages 3% per year, in twenty-four years the purchasing power of your $24,000 will be cut in half to $12,000. Ouch.

Flexibility

The insurance industry has created SPIAs with some flexibility. You can attach various riders that will increase your monthly payments to keep pace with inflation. Also, should you die too soon, some carriers will return some percentage of your original principal, less what you have withdrawn, to your heirs.

When to use an SPIA

Purchasing an SPIA can make sense if you want to cover your fixed expenses during your desirement years. You may have greater peace of mind knowing that a percentage of your lifetime expenses will be paid regardless of what happens to the value of your other investments.

Warning

Never invest 100% of your investments or cash into an SPIA. You'll always need some liquidity or cash for unexpected emergencies and other investments as a hedge on inflation risk.

Fixed Annuity

Benefits
A fixed annuity is a contract that offers you a fixed rate of return on your money for a fixed period of time. At the end of that term, you can withdraw your money, renew the contract, or convert to an immediate annuity and begin taking income.

Historically, fixed annuity rates have been higher than money market accounts and certificates of deposit. They're very conservative instruments. You don't pay taxes on your earnings until you withdraw money from the annuity, so like your 401(k), a fixed annuity acts as a tax-deferral mechanism.

Drawbacks
Most fixed annuities have a back-end surrender charge that can last three to fifteen years. This means that if you take your money out before the term ends you'll be hit with an early withdrawal penalty that varies from company to company. Most companies will allow you to withdraw 10% to 15% of your original investment, or the interest you have earned, whichever is greater, without a penalty. This is commonly known as a "free-withdrawal privilege."

Risks
Fixed annuities are similar to certificates of deposit in that they pay a fixed rate for a fixed term and have no risk. They're not, however, insured by the FDIC; they're backed only by the financial strength of the insurance carrier. Always check the rating of the insurance provider before investing. In addition, every state has a state guarantee insurance pool of $100,000 to $300,000. If you invest $100,000 in a fixed annuity and the underlying insurance company goes bankrupt, the state where that insurance company is domiciled will insure your principal up to the state guarantee amount.

Indexed Annuity

Benefits
An indexed annuity is like a fixed annuity in that it guarantees lifetime income benefits; the difference is the rate of return your money earns

each year. There are an enormously wide range of index annuities on the market today. You must read the features and benefits very carefully to be sure you understand what returns are being promised and for what period of time, and how the returns will be credited to your original investment—that is, how much of the gains of a specific index you'll receive.

In very basic terms, an index annuity promises to pay you a percentage of the gain of a specific index. Let's say your index annuity will match the gain of the S&P 500, up to an annual gain cap of 10%. If the index rises by 14%, you'll receive a return on your principal of 10%. Index annuities also have different terms that stipulate over what period of time—one year, two years, etc.—the index return will be credited to your account. The index annuity, like a fixed annuity, guarantees your original investment even if the market index you have chosen has a negative return. For example, if the index you choose drops by 40%, your return will be 0%. You're protected from negative markets and you benefit from positive markets. Index annuities are for those who want to eliminate market risk but still benefit from some upside potential. I call this the "heads I win, tails I win (with a cost)" approach.

Drawbacks

On the negative side, it's very difficult to determine the real cost of index annuities and to compare the benefits and features from carrier to carrier. This is where a competent and professional financial advisor can assist you.

Variable Annuity

Benefits

Variable annuities allow you to make contributions at any time and for any amount of money each year. As with fixed annuities, your money is sheltered or tax-deferred; however, the value of a variable annuity depends on the investment chosen. Similar investment options offered in a 401(k) plan are available in a variable annuity—i.e., diversification through a broad range of mutual funds, dollar cost averaging, and automatic rebalancing. However, like an immediate or fixed annuity, the insurance company will guarantee you an income for life—i.e., you're protected from losses. But the real benefits of a variable annuity are its flexibility and the guaranteed income or withdrawal riders that most insurance companies offer. These come with three primary features:

1. Guaranteed growth bucket
2. Guaranteed market lock-ins
3. Guaranteed withdrawal or income benefit.

Two Buckets of Money

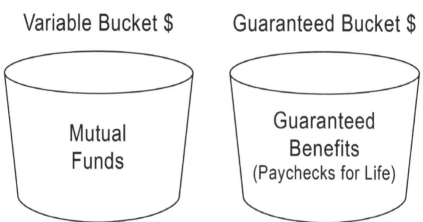

Before I describe each, consider the figure above, which illustrates two buckets of money that represent the two distinct financial mechanisms inside a single variable annuity. Bucket #1 is a variable investment account that allows you to select mutual funds that suit your investment preferences. Think of this as similar to the mutual funds you select in your PCM Co.; the value will fluctuate depending on your investment performance, and you can lose money in this account when you experience negative returns.

Bucket #2 is an account that will provide you with the following three guarantees.

The Guaranteed Growth Bucket

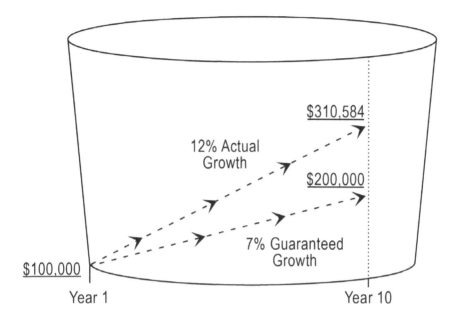

1. Guaranteed growth bucket: Many insurance companies will guarantee to grow your investments by a specific rate of return (5% to 8%). For example if you invest $100,000 and the insurance company guarantees you a compounded return of 7%, in ten years, regardless of what your underlying mutual fund investments do, your $100,000 will have doubled to $200,000. However, if your investment account had grown by an average of 12% per year for that same period, you'd have had a balance of $310,585 in your variable (bucket) investment account.

The figure above gives an overview of how the guaranteed growth benefit increases your original investment by 7% compounded over a ten-year period. If the average return for this period were 12%, your benefit would be even higher.

The Guaranteed Market Lock-In Benefit

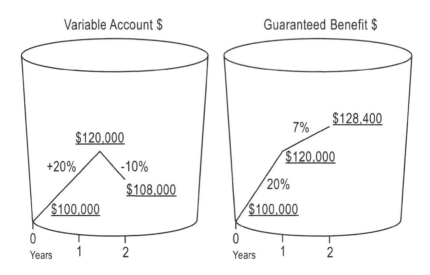

2. Guaranteed market lock-ins: Insurance companies will also guarantee to lock in the gains in your investment account, either on an annual or quarterly basis. For example, if you invest $100,000 in the first year and your gain is 20%, or $20,000, but your guaranteed income benefit is only 7%, the insurance company will lock in that $20,000 on your anniversary, so the value of your guaranteed benefit account will now be $120,000. If the market drops by 10% in the second year, your underlying account balance will be $108,000 ($120,000 − $12,000), but your guaranteed benefit account value will have grown to $128,400 ($120,000 × 1.07). The insurance company is effectively guaranteeing you the better outcome by locking in your investment gains each year and protecting your investment growth from market declines.

The Guaranteed Withdrawals Benefit

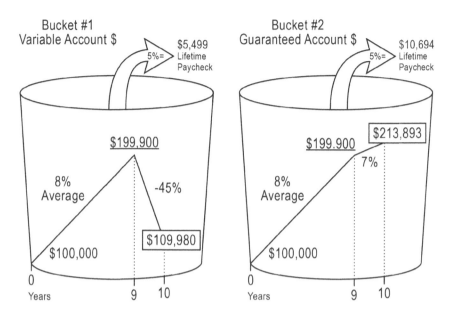

3. Guaranteed withdrawal or income benefit: A third feature is the guaranteed withdrawal benefit. Some carriers will call this the guaranteed income benefit, but I like to call it your guaranteed paycheck for life. This benefit defines the percentage of income the insurance company will pay you on your guaranteed growth account. The percentage will vary by the age at which you begin taking income; for example, from age forty-five to sixty-four, it may be 4%; from sixty-five to seventy-four, 5%; from seventy-five to eighty-four, 6%; and from eighty-five and above, 7%. Each insurance company's income benefit rate will vary.

To see how this benefit works, let's assume you invested $100,000 in your variable account (Bucket #1), and that during the first nine years your money grew by an average of 8% per year. At the end of nine years it would be worth $199,900. Now let's imagine that in the tenth year your investment decreased in value by 45%, bringing your balance down to $109,945. With one negative year your account value is almost back to where you started. (From 2000 to 2010, this is what many investors actually experienced; the credit crisis of 2008 made this period known as "the lost decade" for the average investor.)

Now let's look at Bucket #2, your guaranteed growth account. How did that fare during this same time period? Because the insurance company guaranteed to grow your investment by a compounded rate of 7%, regardless of any negative markets, the value of your guaranteed growth benefit will be $200,000 at the end of the ten years. That's the minimum value the insurance company is guaranteeing. But there's even better news: the second benefit, guaranteed market lock-ins, has insured that your market gains, which averaged 8% per year, have been locked in each year. This has guaranteed that, by the ninth year, the insurance company has locked in the $199,900 value, so when the market drops by 45% in year ten, reducing your mutual fund investments in Bucket #1 to $109,945, the value of Bucket #2 actually grows by the guaranteed 7%, and has a value of $213,893. I don't know about you, but $213,893 looks a lot better to me than $109,945.

By now you're probably thinking, "Charlie, what does this have to do with the guaranteed withdrawal benefit?" Let's imagine you're ready to retire and are interested in generating paychecks for life from these funds. If all you had was the $109,945 in your variable account (Bucket #1) and you withdrew 5% from the account each year (and that's all it earned each year), you'd have an income of $5,497.25 for life.

The good news is that you purchased the variable annuity with the guaranteed riders, and you have a value of $213,893 in your guaranteed withdrawal account (Bucket #2). You're now sixty-five years old and the insurance company, under the guaranteed withdrawal benefit, is willing to pay you that same 5% per year for your lifetime. You will receive $10,694.65 annually—almost double the amount from Bucket #1.

The Guaranteed Withdrawals Benefit figure provides a visual summary of the three guaranteed benefits and the value of your two buckets of money. All three features act as hedging strategies, insulating your investment from the downside market risk and protecting you against longevity risk. In effect, Bucket #2, with its guarantee features, acts like a second parachute, ensuring soft landings for you and your money during significant market volatility.

Drawbacks

The downsides of variable annuities are fees and surrender charges. On average, the fees for the three benefits described above are around 2% to 2.5% per year for insurance and mortality and rider costs. This amount is typically deducted from the value of the guaranteed benefit base, so it includes the guaranteed growth on the investment value. It does not reduce the guaranteed return of the guaranteed account.

Some people think 2.5% per year is a hefty payment. I disagree if it buys you peace of mind. Consider this: hedge fund companies that invest money for the wealthiest Americans use various investment strategies in an attempt to generate a positive or absolute return and insulate their clients' money from market risk. On average, hedge funds charge 2% *plus* 20% of the profits each year for their services. The 2.5% charged by insurance companies for guaranteed annuity features pales by comparison. Security and guaranteed paychecks for life are tough to come by in extreme bear markets. Remember that as the entrepreneur of your PCM Co. you have to balance costs with benefits. This is one cost worth seriously considering as you get closer to your desirement years and your need for financial security increases.

In addition to the 2% to 2.5% fees, you also have to pay the expense ratios of the underlying mutual funds you're investing in. Remember, you pay similar mutual fund costs in your 401(k) plan. This expense is deducted from the sub-accounts you invest in and not the guaranteed benefit amount. You can find these fees in the variable annuity prospectus or in individual fund fact sheets provided by most insurance companies.

Surrender Charges

All insurance companies also have a back-end surrender charge as opposed to a front-end sales charge. The surrender charge and time period vary from company to company, but usually they start at 8% of your account value in the first year, then decline each year by one percentage point until year eight. For example, if in year five the surrender charge is 5% and your account balance is $150,000, you'd lose $7,500 if you took out all your money. Most companies have a free withdrawal privilege that allows you to take 10% to 15% of your original investment or your earnings out each year—whichever is greater—without a penalty.

Liquidity
You always have access to the money invested in the mutual fund-subaccounts of your variable annuity, less any surrender charges. This is the money referenced in Bucket #1. You do not have access to the cash value of your guaranteed benefit account, referenced in Bucket #2. This account's cash value can only be accessed as a withdrawal income (paycheck for life) based on the underlying annual value and the isurance company's annual withdrawal rate, which can range from 4–8% currently.

The Stevens's Solution to Fifty-Nine-and-a-Half Years and Beyond
The reason the Stevens's sat so calmly in my office that cold wintry day in December 2008, while most investors were panicking as global markets dropped 37% or more under the weight of the worst credit crisis since the Great Depression, was because they had already enacted a strategy that protected their PCM Co. investments. The Stevens's solution was a simple two-step process that you can follow as well.

Step One: Target Date Glide-To Fund
Prior to the 2008 credit crisis, The Stevenses had each selected target date funds for their 401(k) investments with a glide to retirement DNA. This meant that by the time the 2008 credit crisis brought the U.S. Equity markets crashing down by 37% or more, their target date funds had already squirreled away the majority of their investments into bonds and cash equivalents. (The funds had started gradually reducing the couple's equity holdings and increasing their bond holdings when each turned fifty-five). In Jerry's case, since he was almost sixty, 80% of

his investment account was in bonds; in 2008, bonds averaged an 8.4% return.

Step Two: Convert to a Variable Annuity Strategy

When Jerry turned fifty-nine-and-a-half in June 2008, the Stevens's and I met to discuss the benefits of a variable annuity strategy. The couple liked the idea of having a second parachute that would guarantee their paychecks for life. We established an individual retirement variable annuity (IRVA) for Jerry and transferred 100% of his PCM Co. to this account. Jerry did not pay taxes on this transfer because the money rolled into individual retirement account. In effect, Jerry created his own personal PCM Co. inside his IRVA.[1]

Linda, at age fifty-five, normally wouldn't have been able to roll her 401(k) contributions into an annuity until she was fifty-nine-and-a-half. Her company's 401(k) plan, however, had an early withdrawal privilege that allowed employees to roll their money out at age fifty-five, even if they were still working. This allowed us to transfer only that percentage of her retirement assets that represented her employer's profit sharing contributions to her own IRVA. Linda had to leave her 401(k) contributions in the plan until she turned fifty-nine-and-a-half. (You must read your 401(k)'s summary plan description carefully to see what options you have for rolling money out of your plan prior to turning fifty-nine-and-a-half.) Both Jerry and Linda continued to contribute the maximum 401(k) and catch-up amounts each year to their PCM Cos. until they reached age sixty-five. This allowed them to continue to receive the maximum matching contributions from their employers (OPM). One hundred percent of their contributions continue to be made to a conservative target date fund within their PCM Cos.

When you add the three guaranteed features of a variable annuity strategy—7% guaranteed growth, guaranteed quarterly market lock-ins, and 5% guaranteed income for life starting at age sixty-five—I

---

[1] As Jerry's personal advisor, I was not an advisor and/or fiduciary to Jerry's company 401(k) and, therefore, not subject to the prohibited transaction rules under DOL Advisory Opinion 2005-23A, which pertain to a rollover of an employee's qualified retirement funds. With regards to Linda's 401(k) plan, our firm provided only non-fiduciary educational services, and again was not restricted by the DOL Advisory Opinion 2005-23A in recommending she roll over part of her 401(k) funds.

think you can see why Linda and Jerry Stevens sat so calmly in my office that bleak winter day of 2008. By transferring a significant percentage of their 401(k) balances into the variable annuities, they had peace of mind knowing that no matter what the market did, negative or positive, their money was protected. They knew it would grow by a minimum of 7% inside the annuity, while the money in their 401(k) plans was in a conservative target date fund. At age sixty-five they'd roll their remaining PCM Co. funds into their variable annuity accounts and begin receiving paychecks for life of no less than 5% of their guaranteed growth account value. Jerry and Linda had greater peace of mind knowing that they each receive a guaranteed paycheck for life, the value of which could not be reduced if the market dropped, as it did significantly in 2008.

The Stevenses' Minimum Guaranteed Outcome

As it turned out, by putting the couple's money into variable annuities, we were able to increase the equity exposure in their investment account from the 20% they had in their 401(k) target date funds to 80% inside their variable annuities, because they knew they were getting a guaranteed 7% growth on their money. Because of this strategy, in 2009 their total return was 28% rather than the 7% we had assumed—and this gain was locked in for future growth. (Note that the performance and strategy the Stevens's chose is no guarantee that you'll experience the same outcome.)

A Second Parachute

One way to think about the guarantees of a variable annuity rider is that of taking an extra parachute with you every time you jump out of an airplane. Would you jump with only one parachute? Even the most skilled professional jumpers have a second chute in case the first one fails to work. Think of a guaranteed benefit rider as a second parachute that's wrapped around your investment accounts. Should the accounts suffer a severe drop in their market value, the guaranteed annuity rider is there to inflate the value of your investment account to a safe level that will continue to provide paychecks for life and protect you from crashing into your desirement years without enough money to live on. Instead, you'll float safely into and through your desirement years.

401(k) Plan Annuity Options

Your 401(k) plan carrier may offer annuity options inside your 401(k) such as the three guaranteed features I have described. If it does, you're the one who must elect to purchase these options or riders. They will not automatically be given to you or mandated by your employer.

Technically speaking, the products offered inside 401(k) plans are not annuities but something generically called "guaranteed income solutions." Each provider will have its own catchy name, such as Prudential's Income-Flex or John Hancock's Guaranteed Income for Life (GIFL). Regardless of the name, because these products behave like annuities I loosely refer to them that way to make it easier for people to understand. Currently, only a handful of companies such as Prudential, John Hancock, and Lincoln Financial Group offer annuity features within 401(k) plans; however, due to the strong, positive response by participants, this feature will undoubtedly become more common. If your 401(k) plan doesn't offer this option now, there's a good chance you'll see it offered soon.

Here's how a typical annuity inside of a 401(k) works. You begin by purchasing a rider from the plan provider. A rider is just a contract for additional insurance, which is typically not covered in a primary policy. Many of you are familiar with riders purchased in conjunction with other types of insurance. For instance, most people must buy riders to protect expensive jewelry, which is not covered by a standard home-owner's policy. The idea is the same here; you're just buying a rider to insure assets inside your 401(k).

The fees used to purchase the rider must come from within the 401(k); you cannot pay for it separately such as with a check or credit card. One of the immediate drawbacks, therefore, is that you sacrifice some of your assets today in exchange for guaranteeing a fixed amount in the future. The fees range from about thirty-five to seventy-five basis points ($350 to $750 per $100,000 in assets).

The years spent paying for the annuity are called the accumulation period or deferral period, and the contract will specify a minimum amount of time. Most carriers require a minimum five-year holding period, which allows the insurer to invest and gain a return on the money.

If your 401(k) plan provider offers a guaranteed income for life type of product, it can be applied to a portion of your assets, just like any investment choice in the 401(k). In other words, you're not required to bind your entire 401(k) to any such guarantee. If you have $50,000 in the plan, for example, you could elect to insure half that amount, or $25,000. It's entirely your decision as to how much you'd like to insure, if any at all.

Advantages of a 401(k) Annuity

Guaranteed paychecks for life

Once you purchase a rider, the insurance company agrees to increase the value of that invested money by a fixed percentage each year. The money in an annuity can only increase in value, never fall. The fixed rate will usually be quoted to two decimal places such as 5.50%, for example, and will vary according to market conditions. As a guideline, the rates will usually be somewhat more competitive than certificate of deposit or savings account rates. Whatever your rate happens to be, it's locked in and never changes.

> **"The money inside an annuity can only increase in value, never fall."**

By purchasing a rider, you continue to leave the protected assets in a mutual fund or target date fund of your choice. The insurer effectively creates a second account—let's call it the insured account—which grows in value by the fixed contract percentage. Once you reach fifty-nine-and-a-half years of age, provided you have met the five-year minimum holding period, you can make a choice:

1. If you'd like to take guaranteed distributions, the insurer will pay 5% of the guaranteed amount for life. This 5% figure is standard in the industry and is independent of your lock-in rate. No

matter what happens to the value of your invested funds, you're guaranteed 5% of the insured account's value per year.

2. If you'd like to tap into some of the accumulated funds, the guaranteed payments are reduced on a pro rata basis.

Let's assume you'd like to retire in fifteen years. You have $100,000 in your 401(k) and wish to insure the entire amount. You purchase a rider that guarantees 5.5% growth and costs thirty-five basis points. The insurer will give you several choices of available investments (which won't necessarily be the same ones available to all 401(k) participants) and immediately charge your account $350 ($100,000 × 0.35). Every year, the insurer takes a snapshot of the mutual fund's value and charges you thirty-five basis points of that value; therefore, your annual charges will vary depending on market conditions.

From now until retirement, your benefit will always be insured. You may invest it in other funds within the insured plan if you choose. At the same time, the insurer effectively creates a second account that takes your starting $100,000 balance and increases it at a steady 5.5% each year (assuming you chose the second option above). At the end of fifteen years, it's guaranteed to be worth $223,247 ($100,000 × $[1 + 0.055]^{15}$)— more than double your starting point. Your guaranteed figure is called the benefit base. At retirement, you'll receive $11,162 ($223,247 × 0.05) per year, for life. You can set up the distributions to be monthly, quarterly, etc., as long as you don't exceed your annual limit. You can't outlive the benefit, a risk known as longevity risk. You have manufactured paychecks for life.

Can you withdraw any of your benefit base in cash at retirement? Most plans allow you to access the cash value of the benefit base; however, you'll reduce your guaranteed payments by the same proportion. Further, most plans limit your deductions to 20% annually. If you, for example, withdraw $44,649 ($223,247 × 20%) in cash, you'll cut your benefits by 20% from $11,162 to $8,930.

While the payments may seem modest, let's not forget that outside of a contract like this there are no guarantees that your account would ever reach $223,247 or above. As we have already seen in previous examples, one good market hit prior to retirement could have a drastic, negative impact. By taking the withdrawal benefit each year you're guaranteed to receive that fixed payment—forever.

Most plans allow you to choose to have the benefit to be paid to your spouse in the event he or she outlives you. If you opt for that benefit, the insurer will reduce the annual payment by about fifty basis points, so you may receive 4.5% each year instead of the standard 5%. The point is that the benefits do not have to apply only to the 401(k) account holder. For a small reduction in payments, you can extend the benefits to your spouse.

If you're noticing that the guaranteed features inside a 401(k) are similar to those offered by a variable annuity outside your 401(k), I can see you're following along. The features are, in many cases, similar. What are different are the level of guarantees offered and the fees charged. Typically, the guarantees offered by a variable annuity are higher than the guaranteed annuity riders inside your 401(k). For example, the guaranteed growth feature in a 401(k) is 5% per year, whereas in a variable annuity it can be as high as 7% to 8%. The guaranteed lock-ins are typically executed on the anniversary of the rider inside a 401(k), while some variable annuities offer quarterly or even daily lock-ins. Lastly, the guaranteed income benefit is typically 5% inside a 401(k) at all ages, while outside it can be 6% to 8% if you wait until age seventy-five or older. Since the guaranteed benefits are higher in a variable annuity, the fees tend to be higher as well.

Insurance

Whether you purchase a variable annuity outside your 401(k) or a guarantee rider inside your 401(k), the insurer is using your funds to help generate your lifetime payments. As you withdraw your guaranteed income, it is coming from your investment bucket (Bucket #1; see page 144). Of course, this is the big gamble for you—and them. In insuring the portfolio, you're making consistent fee payments to the insurer in exchange for a guarantee that your paychecks (income) will never run out before you do. The insurer is betting it will be able to use your money, along with the annual fees it collects, to generate a return sufficiently high to pay you the rates in Bucket #2—and earn a profit in the process. If your investments happen to perform better than the guaranteed rates, you've won the bet. For example, if your original $100,000 investment grew to $400,000 because of your investments, instead of the guaranteed $223,247 (in the previous example), you still have the $400,000 available to you.

So why insure the investment bucket? Well, as we've already discussed, just because you expect your investments to rise to $400,000 (or any other value) does not mean they will. As I've said over and over, the majority of Americans treat their 401(k)s like a casino, which is why, in 2008, the plans became 201(k)s for many. If the market crashes the year before you stop working and your account drops by 30%, 40%, 50% or more, you don't have the time to make up these losses. As Dr. Milevsky says, you've fallen off the merry-go-round at the wrong time. If your portfolio was uninsured, you may not have much choice but to continue working. Swift market downturns, financial panics, terrorist attacks, and any number of other unforeseen factors can cause a substantial decrease in portfolio values just prior to your desirement years—the time you can't afford these losses. In addition, you can't afford not to keep pace with taxes and inflation, so you still need to grow your money during your desirement years, which is hard to do if interest rates are low. (As of this writing, they hovered around 1% to 2%.) In the end, the basic idea behind 401(k) and variable annuities is guaranteed paychecks for life.

Drawbacks

Fees

With a flexible account, the insurer treats your highest daily value throughout the year as a high-water mark. It can never fall below that level and it must always rise by at least the minimum percent (5.5% in this example). Even if you see a 30% market slide one year, your insured portfolio value must increase by at least the fixed percentage. So what are the drawbacks of flexible 401(k) riders? The main one is that costs are higher and usually charge an annual one-hundred-basis-point (1%) guarantee fee on the fund's highest value. Further, the insurer may have additional charges ranging from fifty to sixty-five basis points.

In the previous example, we assumed your $100,000 account was marked to a high value of $110,000 after the first year. Assuming a 150-basis-point fee (1.5%), the insurer would charge your account $1,650 ($110,000 × 0.015). In the second year, we assumed it increases by the guaranteed minimum to $116,050, in which case you'd be charged 1.5% of that amount, or $1,741.

Those fees obviously add up and reduce the money that could be invested, but they also bring a benefit. They allow employees to replace the unknown future with a guaranteed result. Of course, the insurance company doesn't know what will happen in the future either. To make that guaranteed lifetime income stream feasible, the insurance company needs many participants to spread the risk. At retirement, some employees will find it greatly paid to use the insurance while others will find it didn't. That's always the tradeoff for insurance. All who selected the insurance, though, are better off today knowing the minimum benefits they'll receive for life in the future. There's no other way to have that luxury than with annuities.

Financial risk
Another potential concern with individual variable annuities and annuity riders purchased inside your 401(k) plan is the financial stability of the insurer. The good news is the money you put in a variable annuity is invested in sub-accounts of mutual funds and is not part of the assets of the insurance company. Just as the funds in your 401(k) plan are not part of the assets of the company you work for, and, therefore, are not subject to creditor risk or bankruptcy, the funds in the insurance company's sub-accounts are outside the reach of the insurer's creditors. There's no fear of losing your principal if the insurance company goes belly-up. Your guaranteed benefits, however, may be lost or reduced if the company is purchased by another carrier out of bankruptcy.

Portability risk
The biggest downside of using variable annuity rider features inside your 401(k) plan is portability. While most insurance companies let you roll your money out of the plan into an individual retirement account (IRA) and continue the guaranteed benefits at the same cost, what happens if your employer changes your 401(k) provider to one that doesn't offer the annuity features you purchased? Currently, you'd lose the benefits you had been paying for. The portability issues between different 401(k) providers have not been sufficiently worked out, and until they are, I caution you from buying variable annuity rider features inside your 401(k). Buying a variable annuity outside of your 401(k) provides you greater flexibility and control to design the features that best fit you (and your pocket book).

Asset Allocation Strategy

One of the big benefits of using a variable annuity with guaranteed benefit riders is that you can afford to take more risk in your investment choices. For example, if you have invested a percentage of your 401(k) in a bond fund or fixed account, earning 1 of 2% per year, because you want to protect that money from market fluxuations, electing a guaranteed benefit rider, with a minimum return of 7% for the next 10 years, may produce a better outcome. Why leave your money in a balanced fund that's heavily weighted in bonds to provide insurance? If you're now paying for insurance, why doubly insure yourself by holding bonds?

When electing to use a variable annuity with guaranteed features, the objective is to design an investment strategy with a higher probability of achieving greater appreciation than fixed income investments. You are now in a position to take on greater risk in your investment allocation since you have the safety net (your second parachute account) of the guaranteed return, market lock-in, and guaranteed income features. It doesn't make sense to leave your investments in an account that has a high probability of earning a lower rate of return than the minimum guarantee (7%) you're paying extra fees for. In addition, since the insurer will lock in your market gains, you want to achieve the highest return you can. Remember, the insurance company is willing to provide you with guaranteed paychecks for life based on the highest lock-in value of your investment account.

Investment Restrictions

Most insurance carriers will limit the amount of risk you can take in your investment portfolio (Bucket #1). The insurance company is guaranteeing to pay you an income for life. This income will first come from your investment account and then, when your funds are depleted, from the insurance company's own pocket. Accordingly, the insurer has an incentive to make sure your investment account doesn't run out before you do. One of the ways it does this is by mandating the percentage of your account that must be invested in fixed income funds (bonds) and cash equivalents (money markets). Typically, this can range from 20% to 30%. Very few carriers today will let you invest 100% of your money in equities.

Is Insurance Right for You?

As a rule, insurance is most suited for events that have high severity but low probability. In other words, you should insure those events that would cause a great financial burden to you but that are unlikely to occur. For example, people don't buy fire insurance expecting their house will burn down. They buy it in case that happens. Because it's a low-probability event, the cost of fire insurance is relatively low and makes sense to carry.

At the other extreme, it doesn't make sense to insure your home against a broken window. That's pretty common and it doesn't create a financial hardship to repair. Because of the relatively high likelihood, the insurance would cost too much to justify its use.

Severe market crashes are relatively uncommon (low probability), but the losses can be devastating (high financial hardship)—especially if they occur just before your desirement years—so insurance can certainly make sense. The two factors to consider when deciding if insurance is right for you are market risk and longevity risk (your expected life span).

> *"The two factors to consider when deciding if insurance is right for you are market risk and longevity risk."*

In the early years when you're beginning your PCM Co., it pays to take more risks. Purchasing an annuity or annuity feature when you're under forty-five does not make much sense, since time will act as the great equalizer in smoothing out your market returns. Further, the insurance fees over long periods of time may greatly reduce your long-term performance. As you get closer to your squirreling years, however, these features become more attractive.

The second factor to consider is your expected life span. Recall that the insurer pays out 5% of your guaranteed benefit base for life. That means you'd need to live twenty years to recoup all of your money. If you live longer, the insurance was a great deal for you. If not, it was a better deal for the insurance company. A 401(k) plan participant in excellent health who intends to begin withdrawals at age sixty may be a great candidate for insuring his or her funds. Another in failing health who will begin at age seventy may be better off foregoing insurance.

If you have accumulated a sizeable account, insurance may be a sound choice. The decision becomes more pronounced if you're close to retirement. For example, assume you have accumulated $600,000 and plan to stop working in ten years. If you can insure a 7% growth rate, you know your account will be worth at least $1,180,291 ($600,000 × $[1 + 0.07]^{10}$) in ten years.

Based on a 5% payout, you'll have guaranteed yourself a minimum paycheck for life of $59,015 ($1,180,291 × 0.05) every year, or $4,918 per month—for life. By insuring the portfolio, you receive guaranteed downside protection against losses, upside potential from market gains, and lifetime income—guaranteed paychecks for life. If you didn't insure this outcome and the market drops 42% the year before you turn sixty-five (as it did in 2008), instead of having $1,180,291 available to generate a $59,015 annual paycheck for life, you'd have approximately $684,569 (close to what you started with ten years before); at a 5% payout, you'd receive only $34,228 income for life, a loss of almost $25,000 per year.

> *"Remember, you can select the funds you wish to insure; you do not need to insure your entire portfolio."*

Because financial markets, life spans, needs, expenses, and many other factors are uncertain, you should seriously consider guaranteeing your paychecks for life. Remember, though: no risk, no reward. For those times that insurance is warranted, it's still best to diversify your decisions. Don't insure 100% and don't bypass it altogether. Instead, consider insuring 30% to 50% of your PCM Co. account balance (and other retirement assets). Remember, you can select the funds you wish to insure; you do not need to insure your entire portfolio. As your account balance grows, you are locking in your gains periodically and insuring a higher future guaranteed income. This will allow you to glide safely into your desirement years with guaranteed paychecks for life.

PAYCHECKS FOR LIFE ACTION STEPS

☐ Annuities offer a safe strategy for guaranteeing your paychecks for life.

☐ Insuring your PCM Co. investment accounts is like taking a second parachute just in case the first fails to open.

☐ Annuity products and features vary greatly. Before purchasing, read all material carefully to ensure the features and benefits are right for you.

☐ Check insurance companies' financial ratings. With an annuity, you're purchasing a promise that may not be fulfilled for thirty to forty years.

☐ Many variable annuities offer guaranteed riders that will provide a specific benefit until you die, thus guaranteeing you paychecks for life.

☐ A participant in excellent health who plans to begin withdrawals starting at age sixty may be a great candidate for insuring his or her funds.

Principle #9

Take Advantage of Tax Benefits with a Roth

Throughout this book, I have assumed that all of your contributions to your PCM Co. are pre-tax. That is, you contribute a percentage of your earnings before taxes and take advantage of USM—Uncle Sam's Money—throughout your earning years. The result of this strategy is that 100% of the withdrawals you make in your desirement years, as you convert the money in your PCM Co. to paychecks for life, will be taxed.

The big question everyone always asks me is "Charlie, what tax bracket will I be in when I reach my desirement years?" And the answer is (loud drum roll, please): "I don't know, nor does anyone else." Why not? Because the politicians in both the White House and Congress keep changing, and with the ever-changing winds of politics comes ever-changing tax rates.

The Great Tax Myth

Let me share a long-held tax myth. Most people believe that when they reach their desirement years, they'll be in a lower tax bracket. This may be true and it may not. My father's accountant, for example, told him throughout his earning years that one day, when he stopped working, he'd magically be in a lower tax bracket. And that's what my father planned for. He was a very successful executive of a very successful clothing chain, and he made a very successful six-figure income while he was working. When he stopped working, he had saved enough money so that his income (and his lifestyle) wouldn't have to change. In other words, he had enough money to generate a six-figure paycheck for life (Good financial advisor? Yes!).

But something unexpected happened to my dad. He started his desirement years in 1993, the same year that President Bill Clinton raised the highest marginal tax rates for six-figure income earners, like my dad, to 39.5%. Instead of being in a lower tax bracket, Dad was actually in a higher one (Bad accountant? No!).

The truth is it's impossible to know what tax bracket you'll be in when you retire. If your income is low to begin with, it's safe to say that, unless you win the lottery, you'll always be in a low tax bracket. But for mid- and high-income earners, this may not apply.

Luckily, there's a strategy you can use inside (and outside) your 401(k) plan to avoid this uncertainty.

Roth Individual Retirement Accounts

Congress first introduced the Roth Individual Retirement Account (IRA), named after Senator William Roth of Delaware, under the *Taxpayer Relief Act* of 1997; however, the ability to open a Roth IRA didn't take effect until 1998. When Roth IRAs were first allowed that year, they followed the same contribution schedule as traditional IRAs. That is, workers could contribute only the lesser of their taxable compensation or $2,000 per year. That limit was stepped up to $3,000 per year in 2002, $4,000 in 2005, and $5,000 in 2008, where it remains today.

The big difference between the Roth IRA and a traditional IRA is that contributions for the former are not tax-deductible. In other words, you pay taxes today on the dollars you contribute. In return, they're not taxed when withdrawn at retirement, which is still allowed to begin at age fifty-nine-and-a-half. Further, the funds in Roth IRAs must be vested for at least five years, but they're not required to be withdrawn by age seventy-and-a-half.

Advantages of the Roth

First, you pay zero taxes on distributions at retirement. You do not need to track cost bases and other tax information. You simply withdraw the money and it's 100% yours to spend. Also, you can withdraw the amount you have contributed at any time without penalty. However, the portion you have earned through dividends, interest, and capital gains will be subject to a 10% penalty if you withdraw the funds prior to turning fifty-nine-and-a-half or if the account hasn't been held for at least five years. For instance, assume you have contributed a total of $100,000 to your Roth IRA, which has grown to $150,000 at retirement. You can withdraw the $100,000 you have contributed at any time without penalty. However, you'd pay a 10% tax penalty on the $50,000 earned through dividends, interest, and capital gains if you withdraw that prior to age fifty-nine-and-a-half or if the account hasn't been held for at least five years.

Second, withdrawals from a Roth IRA will never bump you into a higher tax bracket. For related reasons, Roth contributions may effectively be larger than for a traditional IRA, depending on tax brackets. For example, if you're in a 28% tax bracket, a $5,000 maximum contribution in 2010 may be equivalent to a traditional IRA contribution of $6,945, since you must earn $6,945 before tax in order to net $5,000 after tax. Since you cannot contribute $6,945 to a traditional IRA, the effective contributions may be larger for the Roth. Therefore, if you think you'll earn more in your desirement years than you do today, the Roth IRA is a good choice.

Third, you're not required to make the minimum withdrawals at age seventy-and-a-half.

Finally, because there are no required distributions, Roth IRA assets can be passed on to heirs. Under current regulations, converting to a Roth IRA can reduce the size of your taxable estate. A conversion could allow for decades of tax-free growth. Also, if you name your spouse as the beneficiary of your Roth IRA, the account can be treated as your spouse's own. He or she could forego withdrawals and pass those assets on to your children, which would allow decades of compounding—tax free—to work its magic.

Disadvantages of the Roth

First, a Roth IRA is not available to everyone. Currently, only single-filers earning a modified adjusted gross income (MAGI) of less than $95,000 annually, or married couples earning a combined maximum MAGI of less than $150,000 annually, qualify. (However, starting in 2010, anyone could convert an existing traditional IRA into a Roth IRA.)

The second disadvantage is that by holding a Roth IRA, you'll miss tax savings during your working years and may not be able to lower your taxable income now.

The Roth 401(k)

In 2009, Congress passed a new law to allow anyone, regardless of their income, to contribute to a Roth inside their 401(k). This is a great opportunity for many high-income investors to accumulate money, either for themselves or their heirs, that will never be taxed.

So we're back to the original question: "Charlie, do I Roth my money—i.e., contribute it after taxes inside my PCM Co.—or do I continue to contribute pre-tax and take advantage of USM today?"

There are numerous Roth calculators, both on the web and probably on your company-sponsored 401(k) website, that will assist you in determining which is a better strategy. The problem with all of these calculators is that they ask you what tax bracket you'll be in at age sixty-five and beyond. Who knows? So here is another way to consider the Roth 401(k) option. First, consider the following analogy. Imagine you're a farmer and you're about to plant a bag of seeds in your pasture. If you had a choice, when would you prefer to pay taxes on the seeds?

The Tax Choice

_____A.   At the time they're planted in the ground?
_____B.   At harvest time when the crop is fully grown?

Everyone (once they get it) chooses option A because why not pay tax on the little seeds going in the ground rather than on the huge harvest coming out? And that's the idea behind the Roth 401(k). It allows you to pay taxes on your smaller deposits today, incrementally (marginal thinking at work again), and then grow a bigger amount, to be withdrawn tax free, over your lifetime. When you harvest your Roth funds, you pay no taxes on that withdrawn money.

The solution is to have balance and tax planning options in the future when you begin withdrawing money from your Paycheck Manufacturing Co. Just as you want a balanced investment portfolio (using a target date fund that glides you successfully and safely into your desirement years) you want a balanced tax strategy in which you have plenty of options to mitigate taxes when you begin taking a Paycheck for Life from your PCM Co.

For Those Younger than Forty-Five

For younger employees (those under forty-five), I recommend putting 50% of your contributions into the Roth 401(k) and 50% into the 401(k). The benefits of this strategy are as follows:

- You get at least half the tax deduction (USM) today.
- You get the benefit of no tax on 50% of your account during your desirement years (also USM).
- You have options that allow you to balance your taxes. That is, if taxes are relatively high when you retire, you can draw from the Roth account first and then take your minimum distribution (starting at age seventy-and-a-half) from the 401(k). If taxes are relatively low, you can withdraw from the 401(k) first and save the Roth funds for later. Anyone placing 100% of their funds in either the 401(k) or Roth wouldn't have these options.

For Those Forty-Five and Older

For folks aged forty-five and above who already have a balance of $50,000 or more in their pre-tax 401(k), I recommend you put your full contribution into a Roth (unless the tax deduction is critical for current income tax planning). You need to fill up the Roth bucket with money that will never be taxed and balance it out with the money you have in your 401(k) that will be taxed. Once you reach that 50/50 balance between the two accounts, start putting 50% of your total contributions into each.

Remember, these are general solutions, and individual circumstances should prevail. Check with your financial advisor and tax accountant to determine which solution is ultimately right for you.

PAYCHECKS FOR LIFE ACTION STEPS

☐ Traditional 401(k) money is contributed on a pre-tax basis. You get Uncle Sam's Money working for you today.

☐ Traditional and Roth 401(k) money both grow on a tax-deferred basis.

☐ At the time of withdrawal, 100% of traditional 401(k) money is taxable, whereas Roth 401(k) withdrawals are tax-free.

☐ Your future tax bracket will dictate which is better: a traditional 401(k) or a Roth. Because you don't know what that will be, take a balanced approach and contribute a percentage to both.

Conclusion

Your Paychecks for Life Annual Maintenance Plan

We eat, sleep, travel, work, relax, learn, play, and entertain. These all require money. Paychecks are essential. You must create a mechanism to generate income once you reach your desirement years, or the paychecks stop. You cannot wait for the opportunity to come to you. You must create the opportunity, make a plan, and stick with it. Now is the time to build a business that will create paychecks for life.

Yes, it's true that you'll continue paying into Social Security, but it should be only part of your plan. I have outlined nine principles for you to follow. These principles create an easy process that allows you to take advantage of OPM and compounding to create a perfect Paycheck Manufacturing Company that will glide you into a secure retirement—guaranteed. Take this opportunity to realize your dreams. You have your 401(k) and now you have the Nine Principles that show you how to turn it into your very own Paycheck Manufacturing Co.

The key now is to implement each of the nine principles. Let's walk through what we've learned together. Then, once a year, use this as a checklist to review your PCM Co. business plan and make the appropriate changes.

■ Principle #1: Act Like an Entrepreneuer

Name your 401(k) plan:

My _____ Paycheck Manufacturing Company, incorporated _____ (date).

The act of naming something makes you the owner of it. You're the boss of your PCM Co., so make sure each year to remind yourself that you're in control of your financial destiny; you're the entrepreneur of this enterprise. No more blaming others for the outcome. The buck stops with you.

■ Principle #2: Determine Your Desirement Mortgage

Make a desirement wish list and estimate your projected maintenance and desirement expenses, then determine your total desirement mortgage and fixed monthly payments. Remember that the desirement mortgage is just like a home mortgage: you want to use a low interest rate of between 5% and 7% when calculating your monthly payments into your PCM Co. Review and update your wish list periodically. Simply go to www.paychecksforlife.org and use The Desirement Calculator to calculate your desirement mortgage numbers and track your progress.

■ Principle #3: Use Other People's Money to Capitalize Your Business

Determine what your employer and Uncle Sam contribute toward your monthly desirement mortgage payment, and review these amounts regularly. Make sure you're taking full advantage of your company's 401(k) matching program and that you're maximizing Uncle Sam's tax deduction.

■ Principle #4: Harness the Power of Compound Interest

Say it with me: 10–1–NOW! Remember that you need to contribute, on average, 10% of your earnings to your PCM Co. If you're not at

10%, be sure to sign up for your company's 401(k) auto-escalation plan, which will increase your contributions by a minimum of 1% of your earnings per year. Try raising this to 2% per year.

Principle #5: Use Technology to Save Automatically

Put your PCM Co. investment and savings plan on autopilot by using the automatic features available in your 401(k) plan. This will take emotions out of the investment process and keep you on track in creating a successful Paycheck Manufacturing Co. These automatic features are:

1. Automatic enrollment: If you are not even contributing to your 401(k) plan, notify your company to automatically enroll you immediately. Be certain your initial contribution qualifies you to receive your employer's maximum matching contribution.
2. Automatic increase: If you are not saving at least 10% of your pay, sign up immediately to have your annual contributions increased automatically each year by 1%. This will increase the value of marginal thinking and enhance the benefits of compound interest for you.
3. Automatic QDIA: Wondering which investment elections to make? No worries, allow your employer to enroll you in the QDIA option, provided it is a target date fund with glide-to DNA. If your employer doesn't offer this option, ask for it. Remember, it's your PCM Co.

Principle #6: Manage Risk by Outsourcing

Reduce your investment risk by outsourcing certain tasks to investment professionals. Choose a target date fund whose DNA will glide you "to," not through, your desirement date. This way you'll start squirreling away money beginning at age fifty-five (if you're not already there). Make sure your target date fund automatically rebalances at least once a year. If not, make sure you elect this feature. You can log on to your company's 401(k) website and do this automatically.

If the markets are down, keep investing through a dollar cost averaging plan. Consider increasing your contributions in a down market. Remember: buy low and sell high. Now go watch the paint dry and enjoy your life.

Principle #7: Control Fees and Expenses

Monitor your company's 401(k) plan expenses. Check once a year to see if the plan has changed your investment options. Find out if a lower-cost target date fund is available. If you're unsure about the investment options in your plan, contact your plan's advisor for assistance. He or she is being paid to help you.

Principle #8: Guarantee Your Paychecks for Life with Annuities

Protect your investment outcomes. See if your 401(k) plan offers an annuity option. Seek advice from the plan's advisor, as these can be complicated features. Remember if the annuity features are not portable—i.e., you can't take them with you if you change employers, or would lose them if your employer changes your 401(k) provider—don't spend the money.

If you're fifty-five, or certainly if you're fifty-nine-and-a-half, consider rolling your 401(k) investments into an Individual Retirement Variable Annuity (IRVA) with a guaranteed income or withdrawal benefit. Shop around and compare company features and prices, as these vary greatly. Seek advice from your 401(k) plan's advisor or other financial professional.

Principle #9: Take Advantage of Tax Benefits with a Roth

Take advantage of the tax benefits of a Roth. Consider investing at least 50% of your contribution as a Roth if you're younger than forty-five. If you're forty-five or older and have the majority of your money in the pre-tax account, start contributing 100% to a Roth account to balance out your account values. This will provide you with tax-free income in your desirement years.

Seek Assistance from your 401(k) Advisor

You may need assistance in doing all of this. Your employer has already hired a financial professional to manage the health and welfare of your company-sponsored 401(k) plan. The 401(k) field has become highly specialized. Financial professionals working in this arena have a great deal of training and experience. They're being paid to manage your 401(k) plan and make sure it's working effectively to meet your financial needs. Take advantage of their wisdom and ask for a free consultation. They should be able to help you make the right decisions.

I know this because, as The 401(k) Coach, I have trained thousands of financial professionals all across the U.S. in this field. All you need to do is reach out to your company's 401(k) plan advisor for help. Bring this book and this annual maintenance plan with you.

If you would like assistance in locating a financial advisor who can help you implement my Nine Paycheck for Life Principles go to www. paychecksforlife.org and click on "find me a Paycheck for Life Specialist."

I am confident that by following these Nine Principles you will be successful in creating a Paycheck for Life and financial independence with reduced financial anxiety. I look forward to hearing about your "paycheck" success!

Appendix

Make Your Desirement Wish List

- What do you love to do as an individual?

_____

_____

_____

- What are your hobbies?

_____

_____

_____

- Do you like volunteering your time, and if so, to what causes?

_____

_____

_____

- If you have a significant other, what do you and he/she like to do as a couple?

_____

_____

_____

- If you had all the money you ever needed, how would you spend it to make you and your loved ones' lives better?

_____

_____

_____

Personal Desirement Paycheck Analysis

---

1. Monthly Expenses

Monthly Essential Expenses

Housing   _____

Food   _____

Transportation   _____

Healthcare   _____

Personal needs   _____

Taxes   _____

Total Essential Expenses   _____

Monthly Desirement Expenses

Entertainment   _____

Travel   _____

Family/Friends   _____

Education   _____

Charity   _____

Other   _____

Total Desirement Expenses   _____

Grand Total Expenses   _____

Personal Desirement Paycheck Analysis

---

2. Guaranteed Income Paychecks For Life*

Monthly Guaranteed Income

Sources

Social Security   _____

Pension   _____

Annuities   _____

Anticipated

Guaranteed Income   _____

Variable Paychecks For Life:

_____

Total Expenses:
(minus)

Guaranteed
Income:
(equals)

Guaranteed
Income Gap:

*Guarantees are based upon the claims-paying ability of the issuing company.

Personal Desirement Paycheck Analysis

3. Filling the Gap

What current assets can be used to help supplement
your guaranteed income?

Non-Qualified Sources

Mutual Funds	$_____
Stocks	$_____
Bonds	$_____
CDs	$_____
Managed Money	$_____
Real Estate	$_____
Other	$_____

Qualified Sources

IRA	$_____
401(k)	$_____
403b	$_____
SEP	$_____
Other	$_____

Paycheck For Life Analysis

Guaranteed Paychecks For Life
(Annualized)

1. Social Security

A. _____ $ _____

B. _____ $ _____

2. Company Pension(s)

A. _____ $ _____

B. _____ $ _____

3. Annuities

A. _____ $ _____

B. _____ $ _____

4. Other

A. _____ $ _____

B. _____ $ _____

Variable Paychecks For Life
(Annualized)

1. Retirement Plans (401(K), IRA's, TSA's, 403(b)'s):

$ _____ value age 65 @ _____ %

Retain Account @ _____ %   Deplete Account @ _____ %

$ _____ $ _____
(annualized)   (annualized)

2. Savings and/or investments:

$ _____ value age 65 @ _____ %

Retain Account @ _____ %   Deplete Account @ _____ %

$ _____ $ _____
(annualized)   (annualized)

THE GAP

GAP ANALYSIS

$ _____ Annual Paycheck to maintain lifestyle age _____

minus $ _____ Guaranteed Paycheck

minus $ _____ Variable Paycheck

equals $ _____ Missing Paycheck

All income sources and returns are hypothetical projections only and are not guaranteed. And changes in contribution amounts & performance will greatly impact future values.

Works Cited

The 401K Coach Program. "The Bear Market Manager: Overcoming the Emotional Impact of Market Volatility and Getting Back on Track to Creating Financial Independence with Reduced Financial Anxiety." The 401k Coach® Program, 2009.

Adams, James T. *The Epic of America*. New York: Simon Publications, 2001.

Belsky, Gary, and Thomas Gilovich. *Why Smart People Make Big Money Mistakes and How to Correct Them: Lessons from the Life-Changing Science of Behavioral Economics*. New York: Simon & Schuster, 2009.

Hewitt Consulting. "Do Fortune 500 Companies Sponsor Pension Plans?" *In Focus: Your Retirement and Financial Management Newsletter* 1, no. 1 (2008): retrieved July 21, 2010, www.hewittassociates.com/_MetaBasicCMAssetCache_/Assets/Articles/In%20Focus%20Newsletter/2008/InFocus_0608.pdf.

Israelsen, Craig. Target Date Analytics <www.ontargetindex.com>

Israelsen, Craig. 7Twelve Portfolio <www.7TwelvePortfolio.com>

Kahneman, Daniel, and Amos Tversky. *Choices, Values, and Frames*. New York: Cambridge University Press, 2000.

Milevsky, Moshe A., and Anna Abaimova. Retirement Ruin and the Sequencing of Returns.

Milliman. "DOL Corrects and Clarifies Qualified Default Investment Guidance." *Client Action Bulletin*, CAB 08-11 (May 9, 2008).

Social Security Administration. "The Future Financial Status of the Social Security Program." *Social Security Bulletin* 70, no. 3 (2010): retrieved February 21, 2011, www.ssa.gov/policy/docs/ssb/v70n3/v70n3p111.html.

U.S. Office of Government Ethics, July 2010. Financial disclosure of Ben Bernanke, 2009.

Index

We invite you to continue your experience with
Paychecks for Life at our website:

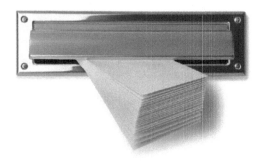

www.paychecksforlife.org

- Share how you feel about "Paychecks for Life Principles" and read what others are saying.
- Share your insights and results with creating a paycheck for life with other readers at the "Paycheck for Life Forum."
- Communicate with the author.
- Read Charlie's blog.
- Purchase additional copies of *Paychecks for Life*.
- Find out the latest news and locations of upcoming *Paychecks for Life* seminars and webinars.

For information about having the author speak to your
organization or group, please contact us at
(877) 932-6236 or info@the401kcoach.com

Charles D. Epstein

has been in the financial services business for 31 years—his entire business career. As The 401(k) Coach®, he has trained thousands of financial advisors and individual investors across the country on his Paychecks for Life System. For his innovative and straight-talking approach, he has been named one of the most influential individuals in the 401(k) industry by 401kWire for four years running.